THE QUESTION
OF
LAY ANALYSIS

THE QUESTION

OF

LAY ANALYSIS

AN INTRODUCTION TO PSYCHO-ANALYSIS

by

SIGMUND FREUD

Translated by

NANCY PROCTER-GREGG

with foreword by

ERNEST JONES, M.D.

IMAGO PUBLISHING COMPANY, LIMITED
LONDON

First English Edition 1947

(First published, in German, 1926)

2 072625 21

H. 12. 10. 56.

BARNARD & WESTWOOD LTD
1-8 Whitfield Place London, W.1

FOREWORD

The question of Lay Analysis, which was the occasion of an animated controversy in psycho-analytical circles some twenty years ago, is one of those on which time exercises a settling influence. The answer to it is determined not so much by personal decisions taken as a matter of policy as by laws, customs, and conditions prevailing in various countries. In some countries, e.g. Austria, Holland, and most of the United States, laws exist which greatly restrict or forbid the carrying out of therapeutic measures by non-medical practitioners; in others, such as France, Germany and Great Britain, the conditions imposed are a good deal more lenient. Apart from laws, however, an acute difference of opinion has obtained concerning the desirability or otherwise of non-medical practitioners. The weighty arguments pro and contra came to full expression in the Symposium on Lay Analysis published in the Official Organs of the International Psycho-Analytical Association in 1927, and they need not be repeated here. In England, that land of tolerance and compromise, we found what has proved to be a fairly happy solution. Recognising that the admission of all lay applicants could only result in the flooding of the profession with lay practitioners and thus alienate it from medical co-operation, we decided to accept only those possessing very exceptional psychological gifts, and we requested the British Medical Association to give a ruling about the conditions under which such work should be carried out. This, as was to have been expected, was that all preliminary consultations and diagnoses were strictly reserved to medical practitioners, who were also to be responsible for a general supervision of the medical progress of the case.

In this brochure Professor Freud puts forward the most powerful advocacy of the practice of lay analysis yet written. Moreover the brochure, written in his most attractive style, contains in addition to the main theme a great many thoughtful considerations which give it a perennial interest.

ERNEST JONES

TRANSLATOR'S NOTE

This short book comprises an introduction to the main discoveries of psycho-analysis, as well as an account of its use as a therapeutic method. It is cast in semi-dialogue form, and the purpose of the discussion is to elucidate the question whether the practice of psycho-analysis should be reserved to medical practitioners. As always happens when a true Socratic spirit of inquiry is present, however, the argument ranges wide and deep; the apparently innocent question cannot be properly considered without examination of fundamentals which at first sight lay far from it.

Thus, an account is first given of typical neurotic symptoms, for which the treatment under discussion is designed. Medicine, hypnosis, suggestion, Confession, change of environment—all are inadequate where neurosis is concerned. Why? What sort of malady is neurosis?

This leads to an account of the discoveries in psychology made by Freud. Just as it is difficult nowadays to imagine how it would feel to hold pre-Darwinian notions, so now it may be startling to realise how recent and surprising was, for instance, Freud's discovery that human mentality functions unconsciously as well as consciously. Failure to recognise this was, as he points out to his interlocutor, the basic misapprehension which prevented psychology from advancing from mere description and unverifiable hypotheses to being a true department of science.

Man's psychical apparatus, as so far discovered by psycho-analysis, is then described in relation to the problem of the nature of neurotic symptoms. Fundamental concepts of the differing functional characteristics of the Ego and of the vaster primitive mentality behind it,

iii

termed the Id, are outlined, and the idea adumbrated that there is a simple formula for the arising of a neurosis, viz., that the Ego has attempted to suppress certain parts of the Id by an inappropriate method (repression), so that these, no longer accessible to the Ego, pursue a life of their own and only reappear on the surface in distorted form.

This in turn leads to a consideration of childhood, since decisive repressions occur in early years when the Ego is weak, and of the springs of human motive. Woven in with the completion of the psychological picture is an account of analytical treatment — the task set, the material and reactions to be dealt with, the methods employed.

All is then related again to the precise question under discussion. A sound administrator was lost in the great psychological scientist, to judge from the acute common sense with which the question of *ad hoc* and unenforceable prohibitions is handled. From what has gone before, it is clear that an analyst requires a long and thorough-going training; should only doctors be allowed and required to undergo this?

At the close of the discussion of this question the window is suddenly opened again upon the wide world. The interests of the patients and the doctors have been considered; what of those of humanity, in its search for enlightenment? If it is true that only those who have themselves been analysed can effectively turn psycho-analytical knowledge to account in other fields of research, where it has already, as in the case of æsthetics, mythology, and the history of culture, begun to be so fruitful—many analysts are needed. Again, if neurosis and maladjustment are to be obviated where they arise— in childhood—analyst-teachers are needed. All this is irrelevant to medicine, and in a noble peroration ('Our civilisation puts an almost intolerable pressure on us...') the author sets the matter in the whole framework of human knowledge and well-being, and leaves it with the confidence he always held that truth will finally make its way, and circumstances be moulded by it.

It may well be that this book, which has not been

published before in England, will be mainly valued as a most masterly and attractive introduction to psycho-analytical knowledge; and as the best answer to the question so often asked, 'What shall I read of Freud?' On the specific subject of the dialogue, however, some practical questions may occur to English readers as to the present situation in this country, and the following facts may be of interest.

Psycho-analysis, as indicated in the text, is a method *sui generis,* and although many expedients are practised by doctors and others under the name of ' analysis ' (and sometimes with the prefix ' psycho ') the only practitioners entitled to call themselves ' psycho-analysts ' are those trained by the Institute of Psycho-Analysis, 96, Gloucester Place, London, W.1. Their professional qualification, which is recognised by the British Medical Association, is Membership of the British Psycho-Analytical Society, which at present confers no diploma but proposes in 1948 to institute a Register. As one condition for admitting a candidate the Institute requires either the study of medicine or some other equivalent previous study or work. The minimum length of the training is four years.

THE QUESTION OF LAY ANALYSIS

An Introduction to Psycho-Analysis

INTRODUCTION

The title of this publication needs some explanation. Lay = non-medical, and the Question is, whether lay persons ought to be allowed to practise analysis. It is topical in both senses of the word. Until now, no one has cared *who* practises analysis. Indeed, far too little attention has been paid to this point, and such interest as has been shown has merely arisen from the wish that *no one* should do so, for which various reasons have been adduced, all arising from the same aversion. The current claim that only physicians should be allowed to analyse betokens, on the surface, a new and friendly attitude towards analysis—always supposing that we need not suspect that it is a modified derivative of the earlier standpoint. It is admitted that analysis is a proper treatment under certain circumstances, but stipulated that only qualified medical practitioners should undertake it. The reasons for this limitation are now to seek.

The question bears a different aspect in different countries. In Germany and America the problem is academic, since there every patient may be treated how and by whom he will, and any 'quack' may set up to treat whatever type of patient he prefers, provided he assumes responsibility for what he does. The law does not intervene unless and until it is invoked in respect of damages

1

incurred in the treatment. In Austria, however, in which and for which I write, the law is preventative, and without waiting for the outcome prohibits persons not medically qualified from treating the sick.* Here, therefore, the question whether laymen, meaning non-physicians, may use psycho-analytical treatment has a practical bearing. It seems, however, that it is no sooner raised than settled, in view of the wording of the law. Neurotic people are sick people, laymen are not medically qualified, psycho-analysis is a procedure designed for the cure or improvement of nervous ailments, all such treatments are reserved to doctors; accordingly laymen are not permitted to analyse neurotic patients, and are liable to penalties if they do so. In this plain state of affairs one might hardly venture to concern oneself with the question of lay analysis. But there are some complicating factors of which the law takes no cognisance, which yet are worth consideration. It may prove to be the case that in this instance the patients are not like other patients, laymen are not, properly speaking, laymen, and physicians not precisely what one is entitled to expect in this connection, and what should entitle them to the claim to be the sole practitioners. If this were so, it would justify a demand that the law should not be applied in this instance without modification.

---

* The same applies in France.

I

The decision whether to modify the law must depend upon persons unfamiliar with the special features of psycho-analysis. We shall assume that such a person has been charged to make an impartial assessment, and that it is our task to supply the information he requires, and we shall assume that those for whom we write are, so far, uninformed. It is a pity that we cannot introduce him as observer into a typical treatment. The 'analytical situation' does not allow of a third person. Further, individual sessions are of very unequal worth, and an uninformed observer on a casual visit would very likely gain no useful impression; he would risk misapprehension of what was occurring between analyst and patient, or he would simply be bored. He must, therefore, for better or worse, content himself with our information, which we shall make as reliable and adequate as possible.

Suppose, now, that the patient suffers from moods which he cannot control, or from despondent timidity which makes him feel his energy is paralysed and he cannot rely on himself, or from anxious embarrassment among strangers. Without knowing why, he may perceive that he finds difficulty in discharging his ordinary tasks, and even in every decision to be made or matter to be undertaken. One day he is afflicted—whence, he does not know—with a painful attack of feelings of anxiety, and from then on it needs a struggle with himself before he can cross a street alone or go in a train; he may even have to give up doing so altogether. Or—a very remarkable thing—his thoughts may take to going their own way, and refuse to obey his will. They dwell on problems which mean nothing to him, but from which he cannot shake free. Ridiculous tasks claim his attention, such as counting the number of windows on the street, and when he does the simplest things, such as posting a letter or turning out the gas, he falls a moment later into doubt as to whether he has actually done them. At first, perhaps, this is merely annoying and troublesome, but it becomes intolerable when suddenly he cannot resist the idea that he has pushed a child under the wheels of a car, or thrown some unknown person from a bridge into the water; or when he feels forced to ask himself whether he is not the murderer for whom the police are looking in connection with to-day's crime. It is obviously nonsense, he knows that himself—he has never harmed anyone; but the sensation, the feeling of guilt, could not be stronger were he in fact the missing murderer.

Or, perhaps, our patient—a woman this time—suffers in another way and another sphere. She is a pianist, but her fingers get cramp and refuse their work. Or, in another case—if she thinks of going to a party she immediately feels the demand of natural needs, to an extent incompatible with a social life. She has to give up parties, balls, theatres, concerts. Or at the most inconvenient times she develops acute headaches or other pains. Perhaps she falls to vomiting after every meal, which if it goes on may become dangerous. It may be that she gets to a pitiable state of inability to tolerate any of the agitations which can never be altogether avoided in life. In such attacks she collapses in a faint, often with muscular spasms which suggest sinister forms of affliction.

Still other patients suffer from disturbance in a particular field, where feelings encounter physical requirements. If they are men, they find themselves incapable of giving physical expression to tenderness towards one of the opposite sex, while all reactions are at their command in relation to objects for which they care little. Or perhaps they are sensually bound to persons whom they despise, and from whom they long to be free. Or their own sensuality imposes requirements on them which they themselves cannot bear to fulfil. If the patients are women, they may be hindered in their sexual life by feelings of anxiety or disgust or by unknown obstacles, or, when they have yielded to love, they find themselves cheated of the premium of pleasure which nature has ordained.

All these people recognise that they are ill, and have recourse to doctors, who are expected to get rid of such nervous disturbances. Physicians have established categories, under which these sufferings are classified. They diagnose them under various names, according to their own standpoints: neurasthenia, psychasthenia, phobias, obsessional neurosis, hysteria. They examine the organs which display these symptoms: heart, stomach, bowels, genitals—and find them sound. They advise a change in the way of living, recreation, a regimen of invigorating exercise and so on, tonics, and achieve a passing improvement, or indeed nothing at all. Finally, the patients get to hear that there are certain persons who particularly concern themselves with the treatment of such maladies as theirs, and they come to them for analysis.

Our impartial inquirer, whom I shall regard as being present, has been showing signs of impatience during this exposition of the manifestations of neurotic illness. Now he becomes attentive, and says, 'Ah, now we shall hear what the analyst will do with the patient whom the doctor could not help.'

Nothing occurs but talk. The analyst neither uses instruments, even for examination, nor writes prescriptions. If at all possible, he leaves the patient's life and circumstances undisturbed during the treatment. This is of course not essential, and cannot always be managed. The analyst takes the patient at a fixed hour, lets him talk, listens to him, and talks to him and lets him listen.

Our impartial inquirer now shows some unmistakeable relief, but also some contempt. He seems to feel, 'Is that all?' Words, words, words, as Prince Hamlet says. And probably he thinks of Mephisto's ironical speech about how one can do anything with words—lines which no reader of 'Faust' is likely to forget.

He says, 'Then it is a kind of magic; you talk, and the patient's malady is blown away.'

Quite right, it would be magic if it worked more quickly. A charm must work quickly—one might say that its results are recognised by their suddenness. But analytical treatments take months and even years; so slow a spell loses all character of the miraculous. We do not, indeed, wish to decry *words*. They are a mighty instrument, the means by which we convey our feelings, the way by which we influence others. Words can do unutterable good, and appalling harm. No doubt, in the beginning was the deed—the word came later; in some contexts it was a cultural advance when deeds were moderated to words. But still, words were originally spells, acts of magic, and they still retain much of their old power.

The impartial inquirer continues, 'If we assume that the patient is no better grounded in the matter of analytical treatment than I am, how do you make him believe in the magic of words or speech which is to free him of his sufferings?'

Naturally, one must prepare him, and it can be done quite simply. One tells him that he is required to be entirely frank with the analyst, not to hold anything deliberately back which comes into his mind, and, as a further consequence, to set aside all the hindrances which might stand in the way of his communicating certain thoughts or memories. Every human being knows that in his own case there are things which he would be most unwilling to tell to another person, or which he would feel it out of the question to tell. These are his 'most intimate thoughts'. He suspects too—and this signifies a great advance in psychological self-knowledge—that there are other things which one does not want to go into with *oneself,* which one tries to hide from oneself, and which one cuts short and drives out from one's mind when they occur to one. Perhaps he observes the beginnings of a very pretty psychological problem in the fact that one of his own thoughts has to be kept secret from his own self. It is indeed as though his self were no longer the unity for which he has always taken it, as though there were something in him which can set itself over against the self. There looms vaguely something in the nature of a contrast between the self and a psychical life taken in a wider sense. If, now, he accepts the requirement of analysis, to tell everything, he will readily expect that an interchange of thoughts under such unwonted conditions may lead to unwonted results.

'I follow', says our impartial inquirer. 'You assume that every neurotic has something which oppresses him, a secret; and by getting him to tell it you relieve him of his oppression, and do him good. That is in fact the principle of confession, on which the Catholic church has so long relied for assuring her power over souls.'

We must answer, yes and no. Confession enters into analysis, as its introduction, as it were. But it is far from being the same thing as analysis, and it cannot serve to explain its effect. In confession the sinner tells what he knows, in analysis the neurotic must tell more. Besides, we have no knowledge that the system of confession has developed the power to get rid of direct symptoms of illness.

'Then I do not understand', comes the reply. 'What does it mean—to tell more than he knows? But I can imagine that you as analysts gain more influence over your patients than the Confessor over his penitents, since you take them for so much longer, and more intensively and individually. And I can see that you use this great influence to dissuade them from dwelling on their diseased thoughts, to talk them out of their fears, and so on. It would be remarkable enough if such methods should succeed in controlling purely physical symptoms, such as vomiting, diarrhœa, and cramp; but I know that such things are possible when a patient is treated by hypnosis. Probably, by the pains you take with the patient, you achieve some such hypnotic relationship, a tie of suggestion to the analyst, even if you do not intend it; and the miracles of your therapy are the results of hypnotic suggestion. But so far as I know hypnotic therapy works far more quickly than your analysis, which you say takes months or years.'

Our impartial inquirer is neither so ignorant nor so much at sea as we had at first supposed. He is clearly trying to grasp psycho-analysis with the help of his earlier information, to connect it with something which he knows already. We now have the awkward task of making it clear that this cannot be done, that analysis is a procedure *sui generis*, something new and unique in itself, which can only be grasped by the acquisition of new insight—or, if one prefers to put it so, new assumptions. But we still owe him an answer to his last observation.

What you have said as to the especial personal influence of the analyst is well worth consideration. Such an influence does exist, and plays a big part in the analysis. But not the same part as in hypnosis. I have to prove to you that the two situations are very different. It may suffice to point out that we do not employ this personal influence—the 'suggestive' element—to suppress the symptoms from which the patient suffers, as is done in hypnotic suggestion. Further, it would be a mistake to think that this element bears the brunt and provides the main furtherance in the treatment. At first, yes; but later it stands in the way of our analytical purposes, and forces us to take most extensive counter-measures. Perhaps I may show you by an example how far the process of averting and dissuasion is from analytical technique. If our patient is suffering from a feeling of guilt, as though he had committed a great crime, we do not advise him to set aside his qualms of conscience on the score that he is undoubtedly innocent; he has tried this himself already, without result. Instead, we point out to him that so strong and persistent a feeling must be founded on something real which perhaps we may discover.

'I am greatly surprised', says our inquirer, 'if by such acquiescence you can silence the patient's feelings of guilt. But what, then, are your analytical purposes and how do you proceed with the patient?'

II

If I am to make myself comprehensible, I must explain to you part of a psychological theory which is either not known or not attended to outside analytical circles. From this theory you will easily deduce what we want of the patients and how we get it. I shall expound it to you dogmatically, as though it were a complete system. But do not think that it came into being as such, like a philosophical system. We have developed it slowly, wrestling long with each point, continually modifying it by constant reference to observation, until at last it has assumed a form in which it seems adequate for our purposes. Only a few years ago, I should have had to clothe the theory in different terms. I cannot, of course, guarantee even to-day that its present form will remain the definitive one. You know that science is no revelation; long after its first beginnings in any field it lacks the certainty, fixity, and infallibility for which the human intellect longs so much. But, such as it is, it is all that we can have. If you take into account, too, that our science is very young, hardly as old as the century, and that it happens to be concerned with the most difficult material that can be presented for human research, you will readily adopt the right attitude to what I have to say. But interrupt me whenever you wish, if you do not follow me or if you require more explanation.

'I must interrupt you before you begin. You say you propose to tell me of a new psychology, but I should have thought that psychology is no new science. There has been plenty of psychology and psychologists already, and I have heard in the Schools of great achievements in this field.'

I should not contest that. But if you examine them more closely, you will find that these great achievements must rather be ranged among those of sensory physiology. The theory of psychical activity could not develop, because it was obstructed by an essential misapprehension. What does it comprise to-day, as taught in the Schools? Apart from this valuable insight into sensori-physiological matters, a number of classifications and definitions of our psychical processes which, thanks to common usage in speech, are now on the tongues of all educated people. That is obviously inadequate for the comprehension of our psychical life. Have you not noticed that every philosopher, dramatist, novelist, historian or biographer arranges psychology for himself, adduces his own particular presuppositions as to the interconnections and aims of psychical activity, all more or less plausible and all equally precarious? There is clearly no common foundation. And so it comes about that on psychological ground, as it were, there is no authority and no observance; anyone may poach at will. If a question of physics or chemistry is raised, anyone without specialist knowledge will keep silence. But if an assertion about psychology is made, everyone feels entitled to express an opinion or to contradict. Seemingly, there is no specialist knowledge in this field. Everyone has his own psychical life and everyone regards himself accordingly as a psychologist. But this does not seem to me sufficient title. There is a story of the woman who applied for a post as children's nurse, and was asked if she understood the care of babies. Of course she did, was her answer, wasn't she once one herself?

'And this common foundation of the psychical life, overlooked by all psychologists,—do you say you have discovered it from observations of the sick?'

I do not think that the value of our findings loses from this origin. Embryology, for example, would deserve no confidence if it could not account for the occurrence of in-born deformities. But I have told you of people whose thoughts go their own way, so that they are impelled to dwell upon problems which are of absolutely no concern to them. Do you consider that the psychology of the Schools can make the least contribution to the elucidation of such an anomaly? And after all, it is the experience of every one of us that each night our thoughts go their own way, and create things which we do not understand, which are alien to us and in significant ways recall the productions of a diseased mind. I refer to our dreams. The common people have always held to the belief that dreams have a meaning and a value, that they signify something. The psychology of the Schools has never been able to say what dreams mean. It has not known what to do with them; if it tried to explain them, it had to become unpsychological, to fall back on sense-stimuli, unequal depth of sleep in the various parts of the brain, etc. But one may say that a psychology which cannot explain dreams is also useless for the elucidation of normal psychi-cal activity, and has no claim to be called a science.

'You are becoming aggressive, and I think you have been touched on a sensitive spot. I have indeed heard that in psycho-analysis great value is attached to dreams, and one interprets them, and tries to find memories of real events underlying them, and so on. But I have also heard that the interpretation of dreams is a matter for the arbitrary opinion of the analyst, and that analysts themselves are still involved in disputes over the art of interpretation, and how far conclusions may be drawn from it. If that is so, you cannot underline so heavily the advantage which psycho-analysis has gained over the psychology of the Schools.'

You have said something very apposite. It is true that the interpretation of dreams has assumed incomparable importance both for the theory and practice of analysis. If I seem aggressive, it is only my form of defence. When I think of the mischief introduced by some analysts over the interpretation of dreams I could despair, and say pessimistically with the satirist Nestroy, 'Every stride is only half the length it looks'. But is it not your experience in other matters, too, that men confuse and distort everything that falls into their hands? With a little precaution and self-discipline one can avoid most of the pitfalls in dream-interpretation. But shall we ever get to my exposition, if we keep allowing ourselves to be diverted like this?

'Well, you were going to explain the fundamental assumption of the new psychology, if I understood you aright.'

I did not mean to begin with that. I want you to hear the idea of the structure of the psychical apparatus, which we have formed in our analytical studies.

'May I ask what you call 'the psychical apparatus' and out of what is it constructed?'

What it is, will soon become clear. As to the material from which it is constructed, I must ask you not to inquire of me. That is no concern of psychology, where the question is a matter of just as much indifference as would be in optics the question whether the sliding parts of a tele-

scope are made of metal or cardboard. We shall set aside
the question of *material,* but not the *spatial* aspect. We
do, in fact, suppose the unknown apparatus which serves
to conduct psychical affairs to be actually like an instrument, made up of various parts—which we call agencies
—each of which performs a special function; and there
is a fixed spatial relationship between them. That is, the
spatial aspect, 'before' and 'behind', 'superficial' and
'deep', only has the immediate meaning of something to
represent the regular succession of functions. Am I still
intelligible?

'Not altogether, but perhaps I shall understand it later.
In any case, that is a remarkable anatomy of the soul or
psyche, which natural philosophers no longer admit to
exist.'

What will you,—it is a hypothesis, and science makes
use of many. The earliest always prove to have been
somewhat crude, and should be labelled 'open to revision'.
I take it that it is unnecessary for me here to appeal to the
philosophy of 'as if' which has grown so popular. The
value of such a 'fiction', as Vaihinger would call it, depends upon how much one can achieve with it.

So, to continue. We take our stand on the ground of
everyday experience, and recognise in man a psychical
organisation which is interpolated between his sensory
stimuli and perception of his bodily needs on the one
hand, and his motor activity on the other; and which
mediates between them with a certain purpose. We call
this organisation his 'I'. This is nothing new—every one
of us makes this assumption, even if not a philosopher, and
some, indeed, even in spite of being philosophers. However, we do not think that with this we have given an
exhaustive description of the psychical apparatus. Besides the 'I' we recognise another psychical sphere, vaster

and more obscure, and we name it 'the It'. The relationship between these two must next occupy our attention.

You may feel dubious over our choice of simple pronouns to designate our two psychical agencies or provinces, instead of high-sounding Greek names. But in psycho-analysis we like to remain in touch with popular ways of thinking, and we prefer to make use of everyday concepts rather than throw them away. That is no merit to us—we must proceed in this way, since our teaching must be understood by our patients, who are often highly intelligent but not always highly educated. The impersonal *it* comes quite naturally into the speech of normal people. 'It upset me' one says; 'it was too much for me.' *C'était plus fort que moi.**

We can only describe things in psychology with the help of comparisons. This is no peculiar feature—it is the same elsewhere. But we have to keep changing the comparisons, for none proves adequate for long. When I want to make the relationship clear between Ego and Id, I have to ask you to imagine the Ego as a kind of façade to the Id, a foreground—an external cortex of the Id, as it were. We may stick to this last comparison. We know that cortical layers, such as the bark of a tree, owe their special characteristics to the modifying effect of the external medium with which they are in contact. So we represent the Ego as the outer layer of the psychical apparatus, the Id; a layer modified by the influence of the outside world (reality). You see from this how in psycho-analysis we make serious play with spatial notions. The Ego is really a superficies, the Id something deeper, when regarded from without. The Ego lies between reality and the Id, which is the psyche proper.

---

* In accordance with the usage adopted by psycho-analysts in England, these terms 'I' and 'It' have been replaced by 'Ego' and 'Id' throughout the remainder of this translation. *Tr.*

'I will not ask yet how you can know all this. Tell me first, what useful purpose is served by this separation of an Ego and an Id?'

That question helps me to see how best to proceed. The important and valuable thing to know is that in several points the Ego and the Id differ sharply from each other. Psychical acts issue in the Ego under other rules than those which apply in the Id; the Ego pursues different ends, and by different means. There is very much that might be said on that, but perhaps you will be satisfied with a fresh comparison and an example. Think of the distinction between the front and the hinterland, as we knew them in the first world war. We never questioned that things proceeded differently at the front, and that much was allowed in the hinterland which had to be forbidden at the front. The operative factor was of course the nearness of the enemy; for the psychical life it is the nearness of the outside world. 'Outside', 'alien', 'hostile' were once identical concepts. And now for the example. In the Id there are no conflicts; contradictions and antitheses exist side by side, and often equalise matters between themselves by compromise-formations. But the Ego, in similar case, feels a conflict which must be decided, and the decision consists in giving up one impulse in favour of the other. The Ego is an organisation, marked out by a very noteworthy tendency towards unity and synthesis; the Id has not this character—it is, so to speak, all in pieces, and its individual impulses pursue their ends independently and regardless of one another.

'And if such an important psychical hinterland exists, how can it have been overlooked until the invention of analysis?'

That takes us back to one of your earlier points. Psychology blocked its own access to the sphere of the Id by holding to an assumption which seems natural, but is in fact untenable; namely, that all psychical acts are conscious, that what is mental is actually distinguished as such by the very fact of being conscious, and that, if unconscious processes do take place in our brains, these do not merit the name of mental acts and are no concern of psychology.

'I should have thought that self-evident.'

Yes, psychologists have thought so too, but it is easy to show that it is false—that is, that it is an inappropriate division. It needs very little self-observation to learn that one may have ideas which cannot have appeared without preparation. But you know nothing of this preliminary stage in your thinking, which in fact must also have been of a mental nature; only the finished result comes into your consciousness. Sometimes you may be able *afterwards,* as by a process of reconstruction, to make these preparatory thoughts conscious.

'Probably one's attention was diverted, so that one did not notice the preparation.'

Prevarication! You cannot in that way get round the fact that acts of a mental nature, often very complicated, may go on in you without your being conscious of them, without your knowing anything of them. Or are you ready to accept the implication that more or less of your 'attention' is enough to change a non-mental act into a mental one? In any event, why need we argue? Hypnotic experiments have demonstrated the existence of such non-conscious thoughts irrefutably, for anyone who is willing to learn.

'I do not wish to deny it, but I think I now understand what you mean. What you call the 'Ego' is consciousness, and your 'Id' is the so-called sub-conscious, so much talked about just now. But why masquerade under new names?'

There is no masquerade; those names do not fit the case. Do not give me literature for science. When some-one talks of the subconscious, I do not know whether he means it topographically, as what lies in the psyche below consciousness, or qualitatively, as another consciousness—a subterranean one as it were. Probably he is not clear on the point himself. The only admissible antithesis is between conscious and unconscious. But it would be a serious error to suppose that this distinction coincides with that between the Ego and the Id. It would be very nice if it were so simple, and our theory would have an easy passage—but it is not so. This much only is correct—that everything which goes on in the Id is unconscious and remains so, and that the processes in the Ego (they alone) *may* become conscious. But they are not all conscious, nor always so, nor necessarily so; and large parts of the Ego may remain unconscious indefinitely.

It is a complicated matter for a psychical process to become conscious. I cannot avoid an explanation—again dogmatic—of our assumptions in this respect. You remember that the Ego is the outer, peripheral, layer of the Id. We hold that on the outermost surface of this Ego is formed a special agency, turned directly towards the external world; it is only through the excitation of this system, or organ, that the phenomenon comes about which we name consciousness. This organ may equally well be excited from without, when with the aid of the sensory organs it receives stimuli from the external world, or from within, when first the sensations in the Id, and then also the processes in the Ego, can be brought into awareness.

'This is getting worse still, and rather beyond me. You invited me to a discussion on whether laymen, meaning people who are not medically qualified, should be allowed to practise analysis. Why must we have these explanations of far-fetched and obscure theories, which I cannot find convincing?'

I know that I cannot convince you. That is outside the bounds of possibility, and so outside my intention. When we instruct our own pupils in theoretical psycho-analysis we notice how little impression we make on them. They are as cool towards analytical teachings as to other abstractions which have been fed to them. Some perhaps wish to be convinced, but there is no sign that they are so. Now, we consider that everyone who wishes to treat others by analysis should first undergo an analysis himself. Only in the course of this 'self-analysis' (as it is mistakenly termed), when he actually experiences in his own person, or rather in his own psyche, the processes asserted by analysis to take place, does he acquire the convictions by which he will be later guided as an analyst. So how can I expect to convince you of the rightness of our theories— you the impartial inquirer, before whom I can only lay an incomplete brief outline, which is obscure on that account, and which cannot come alive in your own experiences?

I am proceeding with a different purpose. The question between us is not whether psycho-analysis is sense or nonsense, whether its theories are right or grossly mistaken. I am setting out our theories for you because that is the best way for me to make clear what is the intellectual content of analysis, what premises it adopts in treating a patient, and what it aims to do with him. In that way an especial light will be thrown on the question of lay analysis. And for the rest be content, if you have followed me so far you have got through the worst, and the remainder will be easier. But you must let me have a breathing space.

III

'I assume that you will give me an idea of how, on the basis of psycho-analytical theories, a nervous complaint may be supposed to arise.'

I will try to do so. But for that we must study our Ego and Id from a new standpoint, the *dynamic;* that is, with an eye to the forces interplaying within them and between them. Up to now we have contented ourselves with describing the psychical apparatus.

'If only this will not again be so difficult to grasp!'

I hope it will not be. You will soon find your way. Let us assume that the forces which drive the psychical apparatus are generated in the organs of the body, as an expression of the great bodily needs. You remember that Schiller said that the world moves by hunger and love; certainly a pair of powers to be respected! We call these bodily needs, in so far as they form the stimulus for psychical activity, *instincts.* These instincts fill the Id; to put it shortly, all energy in the Id comes from them. The forces in the Ego, too, have no other origin, they are all derived from those in the Id. What, now, do the instincts want? Satisfaction, that is, the establishment of situations in which the bodily needs may be extinguished. The lowering of the tension created by needs is felt by our consciousness as pleasurable; a heightening is soon felt as unpleasurable. From these fluctuations arises the series of pleasurable-unpleasurable feelings, according to which the whole psychical apparatus regulates its activity. We speak in this connection of a 'supremacy of the pleasure principle.'

Things become intolerable if the claims of the instincts in the Id can find no satisfaction. Experience soon shows that satisfying situations can only be established with the help of the outer world. With this, the part of the Id turned towards the outer world, the Ego, begins to function. If it is the instinctual forces from the Id which provide the propulsion, yet it is the Ego which does the steering—without which, no goal can be reached. The instincts in the Id press for immediate satisfaction, regardless of all else, and in this way either fail of achievement or actually do damage. It is the Ego's task to avert these mishaps, to mediate between the pretensions of the Id and the preventions of the outer world. It develops its activity in two directions. On the one hand, it observes the outer world, with the aid of its sense-organ—the system of consciousness—so as to seize the most favourable moment for harmless satisfaction; on the other, it influences the Id, curbing its 'passions', inducing the instincts to postpone their satisfaction—even, when it sees that it is necessary, to modify their aims or surrender them against some compensation. In taming the impulses of the Id in this way the Ego replaces the pleasure principle, which was earlier the sole regulating factor, by the so-called *reality principle,* which indeed pursues the same ends but takes into account the conditions imposed by the outer world. Later, the Ego learns that there is another way to make sure of satisfaction, besides the *adaptation* to the outer world just described. One can also come to terms with the outer world by actively *modifying* it, and deliberately create conditions which make satisfaction possible. This activity is the highest achievement of the Ego; decisions as to when it is most to the purpose to master one's passions and bend before reality, or to take arms on their behalf against the outer world, are the alpha and omega of wisdom in conduct.

'And does the Id allow this mastery to the Ego, if, as I understand you, it is the stronger?'

Yes, this happens successfully, if the Ego achieves its full organisation and capacity, has access to all parts of the Id, and can bring its influence to bear on it. There is no natural enmity between Ego and Id, they belong together and in a healthy case there is in practice no division between them.

'I can follow that, but what I don't see is how, in such an ideal situation, there can be any loophole for a disorder.'

You are right; so long as the Ego, and its connections with the Id, fulfil these ideal requirements there will be no neurotic disturbance. The place of irruption for illness is an unexpected one, although no one familiar with general pathology will be surprised to find that it is precisely the most significant developments and differentiations which contain in themselves the germ of disease—of functional failure.

'You are getting too learned, and I cannot understand you.'

I must enlarge a little. A small living creature is a puny thing, powerless against the mighty outside world, which is full of destructive agencies. A primitive being, which has developed no adequate Ego-organisation, is prey to all these 'traumas'. It lives by the 'blind' satisfaction of its instinctual wishes, and often perishes by them. The differentiation of an Ego is, above all, a step towards preservation of life. There is nothing to be learnt from destruction, but a being which has successfully withstood a trauma notices the approach of similar situations and signalises danger by an abbreviated repetition of the impressions experienced in the trauma—by *anxiety*. This reaction to the perception of danger leads to an attempt at flight, which operates for the preservation of life until one has grown strong enough to oppose the dangers of the external world in a more active way, perhaps by aggression.

'This all seems to be far from what you promised me.'

You do not realise how near we are to the fulfilment of my promise. Even in beings who later have an Ego-organisation capable of high achievement this Ego is at first, in childhood, weak, and little differentiated from the Id. Now consider what happens if this powerless Ego feels a demand from an instinct which it wishes to withstand, because it suspects that satisfaction is dangerous, would evoke a traumatic situation, a collision with the outer world; but it cannot master it, because it has not yet the strength necessary. The Ego then treats the risk from the instinct as though it were an outside danger, and makes an attempt at flight; it withdraws from that part of the Id, leaving it to its fate, after having refused it all the help which it normally affords to instinctual impulses. We put it, that Ego undertakes a *repression* of these instinctual impulses. At first sight, this has the successful result of warding off the danger, but one cannot change 'inner' and 'outer' about with impunity. One cannot run away from oneself. By the act of repression the Ego follows the pleasure principle, which otherwise it is wont to correct, and it suffers harm on this account. The harm consists in the fact that the Ego has now imposed a lasting limitation on its sphere of power. The repressed instinc-

c

tual impulse is henceforth isolated; it is left to itself and inaccessible, but this means that it cannot be influenced. It goes its own way. Even later, when the Ego is stronger, it usually cannot lift the repression; its synthesis is disturbed, and a part of the Id remains forbidden ground for it. And further, the isolated impulse does not remain idle. It contrives to indemnify itself for the fact that normal satisfaction is denied it. It produces psychical derivatives to represent it, and links itself with other processes which under its influence are equally severed from the Ego; and finally it breaks through into the Ego and into consciousness with a substitute-formation, unrecognisable in origin, —creating what one calls a symptom. At one stroke we see the real case of a neurotic disturbance: an Ego, prevented in its synthetising activity, with no influence over a part of the Id, obliged to renounce some of its activities in order to avoid a fresh collision with what is repressed, exhausting itself in defence-reactions—largely in vain— against the symptoms or derivatives of the repressed impulses; and an Id in which individual instincts have made themselves independent, pursuing their own aims without regard for the interests of the whole personality, and obeying only the laws of the primitive psychology which reigns in the depths of the Id. If we survey the whole situation it becomes clear that there is a simple formula for the arising of a neurosis; the Ego has made an attempt to suppress certain parts of the Id by an *inappropriate method,* and this has miscarried, and the Id has taken its revenge. Neurosis is thus the consequence of a conflict between Ego and Id, on which the Ego enters because—as further investigation shows—it insists throughout on retaining its adaptability towards the outer world. The opposition lies between outer world and Id, and because the Ego, true to its inmost nature, takes sides with the outer world, it becomes involved in conflict with its own Id. But mark well that it is not the fact of this conflict which brings about the illness—for such opposition between reality and Id are unavoidable, and the Ego's constant task is to mediate between them. It is the fact that the Ego, for settling the conflict, has employed the inadequate method of repression. But this in turn arises from the fact that at the time when this task was presented to it the Ego was undeveloped and weak. Decisive repressions all occur in early childhood.

'You have fetched a remarkable circle! I shall follow your advice not to criticise, since you are only wanting to show me what view psycho-analysis holds as to the rise of neurosis, so that its method of dealing with it can be linked up to that. I could query various points, and may bring several up later. But first I shall try to build on your groundwork and even venture a theory of my own. You have expatiated on the relationship of outer-world, Ego, and Id, and put forward as the factor for neurosis that the Ego, in its dependence on the outside world, fights the Id. Is not the other case possible, in which the Ego in such a conflict lets itself be swept away by the Id, and disowns its obligations towards the outer world? What happens then? According to my lay notions of the nature of mental derangement, that decision by the Ego might be what leads to insanity. A turning away from things as they are seems to be the essential feature of derangement'.

Yes, I have thought of that too, and even think it does so happen, although it would need discussion of very complicated interconnections to prove it. Neurosis and psychosis are clearly intimately related, and yet at a decisive point they must separate. This point might well be that at which the Ego decides which side it will take. In both cases the Id would stick to its character of blind obduracy.

'Then, continue. What hints do we get from your theory as to how to treat neurotics?'

It is now easy to define our therapeutic goal. We want to restore the Ego, to free it from its limitations, to give back the mastery over the Id which it lost as a result of its early repressions. This is the sole purpose of analysis; our whole technique is directed to this end. We have to seek out the repressions which have occurred and enable the Ego to correct them with our help—to resolve conflicts in a better way than by attempted flight. Since these repressions belong to very early years the analytical work takes us back to that period. The way to these conflict-situations, mostly forgotten, which we wish to revive in the patient's memory, is pointed out by symptoms, dreams, and the free associations of ideas which come into his mind. These we must first interpret, translate, since under the influence of the psychology of the Id they have assumed forms of expression quite alien to our natural understanding. We may assume that ideas, thoughts and memories which the patient cannot bring out without a struggle are in some way connected with what is repressed, or derivatives of it. By getting the patient to set aside his feeling of resistance towards telling us these things we educate his Ego to overcome its desire for flight, and to tolerate the approach of what is repressed. In the end, when we have succeeded in reproducing the repression-situation in his memory, his compliance is magnificently rewarded. The whole difference in time proves to be in his favour, and the thing before which his childish Ego recoiled in fright seems now, to his mature and strengthened Ego, often no more than childplay.

IV

'Everything you have told me so far has been pure psychology. It has often sounded strange, or a bit thin, or obscure, but it has been *pure* psychology in both senses. Now, I have known very little about your psychology until to-day, but I have always heard it rumoured that it is predominantly concerned with things the reverse of 'pure'. That makes me wonder whether you have deliberately withheld mention of such matters. And I cannot help feeling doubtful on another point. The neuroses are, as you yourself say, disorders of the psychical life. Such important matters as ethics, conscience, ideals—do these play no part when these deep-reaching disturbances occur?'

I see that you have felt the lack of any consideration of either the lowest or the highest matters, in our conversation so far. But that has been because, up to now, we have not dealt with the *content* of psychical life at all. But let me for once be the one to interrupt, although I shall delay our progress a moment. I have told you so much psychology because I wanted to impress on you that analytical work is a part of applied psychology—and, further, of a psychology which is unknown outside analysis. The analyst therefore must first of all learn this psychology, the psychology of the depths or of the unconscious, at any rate so far as it is known to-day. We shall need this when we come to follow matters further. But now, what exactly do you mean when you talk of purity?

'Well, it is generally reported that in analyses the most intimate, and indeed the nastiest, items of sex-life are talked of in detail. If this is so (although from your psychological explanations I do not see that it need be), it would be a strong argument for only allowing physicians to undertake such treatment. How could one think of putting so much power in the hands of other people, of whose discretion one cannot be sure, and for whose character one has no guarantee?'

It is true that physicians are invested with certain rights in the sexual sphere; and they may even examine the genitals. In the East, indeed, this used not to be allowed, and some idealist reformers—you will know who I mean —have contested these rights. But you wish to know whether sexual matters are dealt with in analysis, and if so, why it is necessary? It is, in fact, so.

But it must be so; in the first place, because analysis is built on complete frankness. It involves, for example, open discussion of financial matters, and the patient says things which he would not tell a fellow citizen, let alone a competitor or an income-tax inspector. I would not for a moment contest the proposition that this puts the analyst under great moral responsibility for observing confidence —I would earnestly stress it. And secondly it must be so, because among the causes of and occasions for neurotic complaints sexual factors play an important, an over-weening—even perhaps a specific—rôle. What else can analysis do but concern itself with the material which the patient brings to it? The analyst never encourages the patient into the sexual field, he does not say in advance,

'we must deal with the intimacies of your sexual life'!
He lets him begin his communications where he likes,
waiting quietly until he himself touches on sexual matters.
I have always warned my pupils that our opponents pro-
claim that we shall come across cases where sexuality
plays no part, and we must be strictly on our guard
against introducing it into an analysis, lest we miss the
chance of finding such a case. None of us has so far had
this good fortune.

I know, of course, that the recognition we afford to
sexuality is—whether they confess it or not—the strongest
motive for our opponents' hostility to psycho-analysis.
But are we to let ourselves be shaken on that account?
It only shows us how neurotic our whole cultural life is,
when people apparently normal behave no differently
from neurotics. At a time when learned societies in Germany used to sit in judgment on psycho-analysis (to-day
they are less vocal), one speaker claimed especial authority because, according to his own account, he, too, let his
patients talk about themselves. Apparently he did so for
purposes of diagnosis, and in order to test analytical asser-
tions. But, he added, if they began to talk about sexual
matters, he shut them up at once. What do you think
of an experimental procedure such as that? The learned
audience applauded the speaker, instead of being ashamed
for him. His logical inanity can only be accounted for by
his triumphant security in the consciousness that everyone was as prejudiced as he. In later years, some of my
one-time pupils yielded to the wish to free humanity from
the yoke of sexuality which psycho-analysis is supposed to
lay upon it. One of them propounded the thesis that
sexual does not mean sexuality but something else, something abstract and mystical; a second maintained that the
sexual aspect of life is only one of the spheres in which

man finds scope for expressing his instinctual need for power and domination. They have met with much acclaim—at first, at least.

'But on that, even I would take sides. It seems to me far-fetched to maintain that sexuality is not a natural and primary need of living creatures, but an expression of something else. One has only to think of the animals.'

That makes no difference. There is no mixture, however absurd, that society would not willingly swallow if it seems to be an antidote against the feared supremacy of sex.

I must remark, by the bye, that the aversion you have shown to admitting sex as playing so great a part in the causation of neuroses does not seem to me very compatible with your rôle of impartial investigation. Do you not feel that this antipathy may make it difficult for you to arrive at a right conclusion?

'I am sorry to hear you say so. Your confidence in me seems shaken. Why did you not select someone else for the purpose?'

Because he would have thought no differently from you. But suppose he had been prepared from the outset to admit the significance of sex, everyone would have cried out that he was not impartial at all, but a follower of mine. No, I am not giving up the expectation that I shall be able to influence your views. But I know that over this I am in different case from what has gone before. Over my psychological explanations I had to take the stand that it did not matter whether you believed in what I said or not, so long as you thought we were dealing with purely psychological problems. But now, over the question of sexuality, I should like to be able to make you see that your strongest motive for not accepting what I say is that predetermined hostility which you share with so many others.

'I am still not in possession of the evidence which has given you such unshakeable certainty.'

Quite so, and I will go on with my case.   Sexuality is not just a piquant affair, but a serious problem in the scientific sense.   There was much new to learn, and many singular things to elucidate.   I have already said that an analysis must go back to the patient's early childhood, because it was then, while the Ego was weak, that the decisive repressions occurred.   But it was supposed that there is no sexuality in childhood—its onset occurs at puberty.   We discovered that this is not so; the sexual instinctual impulses accompany life from birth, and it is just these instincts against which the infantile Ego undertakes defence by repressions.   A remarkable coincidence, is it not, that even the small child strives against the might of sexuality, just as in later days the speaker at the learned society, and my pupils who have brought forward theories of their own?   How has this come about?   The widest generalisation would be that culture has been built up at the expense of sexuality, but there is a great deal else to be said as well.

The discovery of childish sexuality is one of those for which one is expected to blush.   Some children's specialists have always, it seems, known of it, as have some children's nurses.   Wiseacres who call themselves children's psychologists at once raised an outcry over 'destroying the innocence of childhood'.   Always sentiment in place of argument!   It happens every day in political affairs. Some member of the Opposition gets up and denounces some piece of maladministration in the civil service, army or the judiciary; whereat someone else, usually on the Government side, explains that such allegations are aspersions on the honour of the State, the military, or the dynasty, or even the nation. So the implication is that they cannot be true. These feelings of honour can stand no aspersion.

A child's sexual life is naturally different from that of an adult. The sexual function undergoes a complicated development between its beginnings and the final form which we recognise as familiar. It grows together out of a number of component instincts with special aims, and passes through several phases of organisation, until finally it is brought into the service of reproduction. The individual component-instincts are not all equally useful for the final purpose, and they must be diverted, remodelled, and in part suppressed. Such a far-reaching development is not always faultlessly carried out, and there may be inhibitions of development and partial fixations at early stages; where, later, the exercise of the sexual function is met by hindrances, the sexual striving—the libido, as we say—reverts to such earlier points of fixation. The study of childhood sexuality, and its changes on the way to maturity, has also given us the key to the understanding of the so-called sexual perversions—which were always described with every indication of abhorrence, but the origin of which no one could explain. The whole field is extremely interesting, but for the purpose of our discussion there is little point in my telling you more about it. To find one's way about it one not only needs, as you would expect, a knowledge of anatomy and physiology, which unfortunately cannot be entirely got in the medical schools; acquaintance with the history of culture and with mythology is also necessary.

'But I still cannot form a real notion of the sexual life of children.'

Then I must dwell a little longer on the subject; indeed I should be sorry to leave it here. I must tell you that the most remarkable feature—as it seems to me—in children's sexual life is that it runs its whole far-reaching course in the first five years of life. From then on, until puberty, it goes through the so-called latency period, in which, normally, sexuality makes no progress; on the contrary, the sexual strivings diminish in strength, and much that the child practised or knew before is given up and forgotten. In this period, after the early blooming of sexual life has withered, are built up such attitudes of the Ego as shame, disgust, and morality, destined to stand against the later storms of puberty and to direct the paths of the freshly-awakened sexual desires. This so-called *double onset of sexual life* has much to do with the rise of neurotic ailments. It seems to be found only in Man; perhaps it is one of the conditions of humanity's privileged status, that man may become neurotic. Before psycho-analysis the early period of sexuality had been overlooked, just as had been, in another field, the background to conscious psychical activity. You may suspect —and rightly so—that the two things are intimately connected.

I could say a great deal about the content, expression, and achievement of this early period of sexuality—all of it unexpected. As an instance: you will no doubt be surprised to hear that little boys are very frequently frightened by the idea that their father will eat them. (And you may also be surprised that I list this fear among the manifestations of sexuality.) But I would remind you of the mythological story, which you may remember from your schooldays, that the god Cronos, too, devoured his children. Surely that story surprised you, when you first heard it? But I suppose we none of us thought much about it at the time. To-day we can think of other tales in which a devouring animal appears, such as the wolf in Little Red Riding Hood, and we recognise the father in disguise. I am taking this opportunity to impress on you that the world of myths and fairy-tales first became intelligible through the understanding of children's sexual life. That has been achieved as a side-issue by psychoanalytical studies.

I anticipate that you will be no less surprised to hear that a male child commonly suffers from anxiety lest his father rob him of his male member; and so castration-anxiety is one of the strongest influences on the development of his character, and decisive for his sexual tendencies later. Here, too, mythology may help you to believe what psycho-analysis says. The same Cronos who devoured his children also emasculated his father, and suffered the same revenge at the hands of his own son Zeus, who had been saved by his mother's cunning. If you have been feeling inclined to think that everything which psycho-analysis says about children's early sexuality arises from the wild phantasy of analysts, you will at least admit that this phantasy has created the same productions as did the imagination of primitive man, as seen in the precipitate of myths and fairy-tales. The other, more friendly, and probably more fitting hypothesis would be that even to-day these same archaic elements are in evidence in the psychical life of children—the elements which dominated human culture in primitive times. The child would thus repeat in its psychical development, in abbreviated form, the history of its psychical descent just as physical evolution is recapitulated, as has long been taught by embryologists.

A further characteristic of the sexuality of early childhood is that the female organ as yet plays no part in it—

the child has not yet discovered it. All the accent falls on the male organ, and all interest is concentrated on whether it is present or not. We know less of the sexual life of little girls than of little boys. We need not be abashed on this account; the sexual life of grown-up women, too, is still a 'dark continent' for psychology. But we have learnt that the small girl feels sensitive over the lack of a sex organ equal to the boy's, and holds herself to be inferior on that account; and that this 'penis-envy' gives rise to a whole series of characteristic feminine re-actions.

Another feature in childhood is that both excremental needs are invested with sexual interest. Education later makes a sharp distinction, but jokes obscure it again. The subject may seem unpleasant to us, but it is well known that it takes children quite a long time to develop a sense of disgust. Even those who otherwise insist upon the seraphic purity of childhood have not denied this fact.

But no fact has more claim to our attention than this— that a small child's sexual wishes are regularly directed towards those who stand in closest relationship to it; in the first place, its father and mother, and beyond them its brothers and sisters. For a boy, the mother is the first love-object, for a girl the father, so far as a bisexual dis-position does not call also for the reverse attitude at the same time. The other parent is felt to be a disturbing rival, and is not seldom regarded with acute enmity. Understand me—I am not saying that the child only wishes for such expressions of tenderness from the pre-ferred parent as we grown-ups are so ready to see as the essence of the relationship between parent and child. No, analysis leaves no doubt on the point that, beyond this tenderness, a child's wishes aspire to what we call sensual satisfaction,—so far, that is, as the child's ideas go on the subject. It is readily understandable that a child never guesses the real facts of sexual intercourse; it substitutes other ideas derived from its own experiences and feelings. Usually its wishes culminate in the idea of bearing a child, or begetting one in some vague way. Even a boy, in his ignorance, does not exclude the wish to bear a child. We call this whole framework the *Œdipus complex,* after the famous Greek legend. At the end of the first sexual period it should normally be relinquished, largely demolished and altered—and the results of this transformation are destined to procure great achievements in later psychical life. But as a rule the transformation is not thorough-going enough, and in that case puberty calls the complex back to life, and its revival may have serious consequences.

I am surprised that you have not spoken yet. It can hardly mean that you accept what I say. When analysis asserts that the child's first choice of an object to love is thus *incestuous,* to use the technical term, it has once more impugned humanity's most sacred feelings, and may expect to be received with corresponding disbelief, contradiction, and denunciation. This, indeed, has been abundantly its lot. Nothing has more alienated the goodwill of contemporary opinion than the demonstration of the Œdipus complex as a common and fated human formation. The Greek myth, indeed, must have meant the same thing, but the majority of people to-day—learned or not —prefer to believe that nature has implanted an innate abhorrence in us, as a defence against the possibility of incest.

But history comes to our help here. When Julius Caesar arrived in Egypt he found the young Queen Cleopatra, who was soon to mean so much to him, married to her younger brother Ptolemy. That was nothing peculiar in the Egyptian dynasty; the Ptolemies, originally Greek, had only continued the practice followed for some thousands of years by their predecessors, the Pharaohs. But that was only incest between brother and sister, which even in our times is regarded comparatively leniently. Let us turn to our best witness for the relationships of primitive times—mythology. The myths of all peoples, not only the Greeks, overflow with tales of loves between father and daughter, and even mother and son. Cosmology as well as the genealogy of royal houses was founded on incest. Why do you think these tales were invented? To brand gods and kings as criminals, and to bring on them the abhorrence of mankind? Rather, because incestuous wishes are an ancient human heritage, never entirely overcome, so that men still wanted to endow the gods and their descendants with their fulfilment, although the majority of ordinary mortals must renounce them for themselves. It is quite in keeping with these teachings of history and mythology that we should find incestuous wishes still present and active to-day in the childhood of the individual.

'I might take it amiss that you meant to withhold all this about childhood sexuality from me. It seems to me very interesting in its bearings on primitive history.'

I was afraid that it would make us lose sight of our purpose. But perhaps it will have its advantages.

'But now tell me, what real certainty have you for your analytical findings as to children's sexuality? Does your conviction merely rest on the coincidences with mythology and history?'

By no means. It rests upon direct observation. It was like this: we first deduced the content of sexuality in childhood from the analysis of adults, that is, anything from twenty to forty years later. But later on we undertook the analysis of children themselves, and it was no small triumph to find that everything turned out to be just as we had inferred it, in spite of the overlayings and distortions of the intervening years.

'Have you really analysed small children, less than six years old? Does that work, and is it not risky for the child?'

It works very well. It is hardly credible—how much is happening in a small child of four or five. Children's minds are very quick at that age; the springtime of sexuality is a time of intellectual blooming too. I am inclined to think that when they enter on the latency period they become mentally inhibited, duller. Many children, too, begin then to lose their physical charm. And as to harm from early analysis, I can tell you that the first child on whom the experiment was tried, now nearly twenty years ago, has since grown up to be a healthy and able young man, who in spite of severe psychical traumas passed through his puberty without any trouble. I have every hope that other 'victims' of early analysis will fare no worse. There are many points of interest about these analyses of children; it may be that in the future they will acquire even greater significance. Their value for theoretical progress is beyond question. They afford indubitable evidence on questions which cannot be decided from the analysis of adults, and so safeguard the analyst against errors which might prove serious. One surprises the factors which cause neurosis at their very work, and one cannot mistake them. In the child's interests indeed, analytical influence must be combined with educational measures. This technique has yet to be perfected. But there is a considerable practical interest in the fact that observation shows that a very large number of our children undergo a definitely neurotic phase in their development. Since we came to see more clearly we have been tempted

to say that childhood neurosis is not the exception but the
rule; it is as though it were unavoidable in the passage
from the infantile disposition to conformity with the culture achieved by society. In most cases, these neurotic
spells of early years are overcome spontaneously; it may
be that their traces are usually left even in those of average
mental health. But on the other hand we never fail to
find, in those who are later neurotic, the connection with
the childhood attack, which usually seems not to have
been very obvious at the time. I believe that physicians
assert, in an entirely analogous way, that everyone in his
childhood is subject to a tubercular infection. There is,
however, no question of inoculation by early neurosis—it
only establishes predisposition.

I will return to your question about our evidence. We
have, as I say, obtained from direct analytical observation
of children the general conviction that we have correctly
interpreted the communications of adults about their
childhood. But in a series of cases another kind of con-
firmation became available. We had reconstructed, from
the material of the analysis, certain outside happenings
and impressive events of childhood years, of which the
patient's conscious memory retained nothing; and in for-
tunate circumstances, from information supplied by
parents or nurses, we obtained irrefutable proof that the
things, which we had inferred, had in fact happened just
so. That, naturally, could not be brought about very
often, but when it was it was extremely impressive. I
should tell you that a correct reconstruction of such forgotten childhood experiences always has great therapeutic
effect, whether it can also be confirmed from outside
sources or not. These occurrences, of course, derive their
significance from their having happened so early, at a

D

time when they could traumatically affect the as yet puny Ego.

'And what sort of occurrences are they, which you must unearth in analysis?'

They are of various kinds. Most directly, impressions of such a nature as to exert lasting influence on the child's budding sexual life. For example, observations of sexual relations between adults, or a child's own sexual experience with an adult or another child—and this does not happen so seldom as one would suppose. Further afield, the hearing things said, which the child either grasped at the time, or only understood later, but in either case took for information about secret and sinister things. Further, the child's own behaviour and practices, which evince a significantly tender or hostile attitude on its part towards other persons. It is of especial importance in an analysis to recall a child's own forgotten sexual indulgence, together with the interference of adults which put an end to it.

'This is where I may ask a question which I have wanted to put for some time. What is this 'sexual indulgence' of a child in this early period, which according to your account was overlooked until the appearance of analysis?'

The usual and main feature of it was not overlooked, remarkable to say; that is, it was really not remarkable at all, for it was impossible to overlook it. A child's sexual impulses find their main outlet in gratification on its own body, by stimulation of its own genitals—in actual fact, the male component of the genitals. Grown-ups have always known how extraordinarily widespread this 'bad habit' is; the habit itself has been considered a sin, and strictly suppressed. Do not ask me how this observation of immoral inclinations in children (for a child does it because, as it says itself, it enjoys it) could be reconciled with their alleged inborn purity and innocence. This riddle must be left for our opponents. For us there is a more important problem. What attitude ought we to take towards the sexual indulgence of early childhood? We have become aware of the responsibility we incur by suppressing it, and yet we cannot assume that it is right to allow it unchecked. It appears that among races of low culture, and in the lower strata of civilised peoples, children's sexuality is allowed free play. That probably constitutes a strong protection against later lapses into individual neurosis, but is there not at the same time great detriment to the aptitude for cultural achievement? There is a good deal which goes to suggest that in this respect we are between a new Scylla and Charybdis.

But I shall leave you to judge whether the interests roused by the study of the sexual life of neurotics are likely to create an atmosphere favourable to licentiousness.

V

'I think I understand your purpose. You are trying to show me what knowledge is required for the practice of psycho-analysis, so that I may judge from that whether it should be allowed only to physicians. Now, so far, little has emerged of a medical nature; we have had much psychology and a certain amount of biology or the science of sex. But perhaps we have not come to the end yet?'

No indeed, there are still gaps to be filled. May I ask you something? Will you now give me the idea you have so far formed of analytical treatment? As though you yourself had to undertake one?

'Well, that may be beyond me. I certainly don't intend to settle the question between us by such an experiment. But I will do as you suggest and the blood be on your own head. Now to begin: the patient comes to see me and complains of his troubles. I promise him a cure, or at least an improvement, if he will follow my instructions. I require that he shall tell me with the greatest frankness what he knows and what occurs to him, and he must not depart from this resolution even if things come up which seem unsuitable for telling. Have I got the rule right?'

Yes. You should add, 'even if what occurs to his mind seems unimportant or nonsensical'.

'Very well, that too. Then he begins to talk and I listen. Yes, and then? From the things he says I guess what impressions, experiences, and wishes he has repressed because they occurred at a time when his Ego was still weak and was frightened at them, instead of joining issue with them. When he has heard this from me, he puts himself back into the situations where it all happened, and with my help solves them better. Then the limitations on nis Ego vanish, and he is restored to health. Is that right?'

Bravo! I see they will be able to reproach me yet again for having made a non-medical man an analyst. You have taken it all in very well.

'I have only repeated what I have heard from you, as one says something off by heart. I still cannot imagine just how I should do it, and I do not understand at all why the work should take an hour a day for so many months. An ordinary man does not as a rule have such a great deal of experience, and what is repressed in childhood is probably the same in all cases.'

There are still all sorts of things to be learnt in the actual practice of analysis. For example: you would find it by no means so simple to draw conclusions, from the patient's communications, as to the events which he has forgotten and the instinctual impulses he has repressed. He will tell you something which on the face of it makes as little sense to you as it does to him. You have to be ready to deal with the material which he brings up in analysis, according to the rule, in a quite special way. It is like an ore, from which the valuable metal must be extracted by a certain process. You will expect that many tons must be treated, and they may only hold a little of the precious metal sought for. This is the first reason for the length of analytical treatment.

'But—to stick to your comparison—how is the raw
material reduced?'

One assumes that the patient's communications and
ideas are only distortions of what is sought—allusions, as
it were, from which you have to guess what is hidden be-
neath. In a word, you must first *interpret* the material,
be it memories, ideas, or dreams. You will of course do
this in the light of the anticipations you have formed,
thanks to your practised knowledge, while you listened to
the patient.

'Interpret! An ugly word. I don't like to hear it, for
it destroys all certainty. If everything is to depend on
my interpretation, who is to say whether I interpret correctly? Everything is left to my arbitrary notions.'

Gently—it is not so bad as that. Why should you except your own mental processes from the validity you are
prepared to allow for others? If you have achieved a
certain self-discipline, and a certain knowledge, your interpretations will not be influenced by personal factors,
and will go right. I do not say that the analysts's personality is of no moment for this part of the analysis. A certain 'fine ear' is required, in discovering what is unconscious and repressed, and not everyone possesses it to the
same degree. And above all, in this connection we see
the necessity for the analyst to fit himself to deal without
prejudice with the analytical material, by undergoing a
thorough analysis himself. Certainly there remains the
'personal equation' to be allowed for,—the same sort of
thing as is reckoned with in astronomical observations;
the individual element will always play a greater part in
psycho-analysis than elsewhere. An abnormal man may
become an accurate physicist, but as an analyst he would
be hampered by his own abnormality in construing
psychical matters aright. Since no one can prove to

another man that he is abnormal, unanimity in matters of depth-psychology is especially difficult to achieve. Some psychologists maintain on that account that there is no hope of such a thing, and that every fool has an equal right to put forward his folly for wisdom. But I confess to greater optimism. Our experiences go to show that even in psychology a fair amount of agreement is possible. Every field of research has its especial difficulties, and it is our business to try to eliminate them. In any case, in the analytical art of interpretation, as elsewhere, there is something of trained knowledge to be acquired, as for example, in the field of indirect representation by symbols.

'Well, I have no further desire to undertake an analytical treatment, even in imagination. Who knows how many surprises might still lie in store for me!'

You are quite right to give up any such idea. You see how much training and practice would still be required. When you had found the correct interpretations, a fresh problem would confront you. You must await the right moment for telling your patient your conclusions, if you are to get successful results.

'And how does one know the right moment?'

That involves a sense of timing, which may become very acute with experience. You would make a grave mistake if—perhaps in an effort to shorten the analysis—you were to throw your interpretations at the patient's head so soon as you had found them. You would evoke resistance, rejection, resentment—but you would not succeed in enabling his Ego to get possession of what was repressed. The prescription is to wait, until he himself has got near enough to it to need only a few small steps further, which he can take under the guidance of your interpretations.

'I think I should never learn to do all that. But suppose I had followed all these precautions with my interpretation, what then?'

Then you are destined to make a discovery for which you are quite unprepared.

'And what is that?'

That you have been deceived in your patient, that you cannot count at all on his co-operation and compliance, that he is ready to put every possible obstacle in the way of your joint task; in a word, that he does not want to become well at all.

'That is the most outrageous thing you have told me yet! And I don't believe it. The patient who suffers so much, who complains so genuinely, who sacrifices so much to the treatment—he doesn't want to get well! You cannot mean it.'

You must take it that I do mean it. What I said was the actual truth—not the whole truth, but a noteworthy part of it. The patient does want to get well, but also he does not want to. His Ego has lost its unity, so it has no single-minded purpose. If he were otherwise, he would not be a neurotic.

The derivatives of what is repressed have broken through into the Ego and are asserting themselves there; and the Ego has as little mastery over the impulses of this origin as over the repressed impulses themselves—and commonly is as little aware of them. These patients indeed are of a special kind, and difficulties arise with which we do not usually have to reckon. All our social institutions are cut to the pattern of people with a unified, normal Ego, which one can classify as good or bad, and which either fulfils its function or is disabled by an overpowering influence. Hence the juridical alternative—responsible or not responsible. But these distinctions do not fit the case of neurotics. One must admit that it is difficult to adapt the demands of society to their psychology. This became very obvious during the great war. Were neurotics who evaded military service simulating unfitness or not? They were both. If they were treated as pretending, and their illness made thoroughly uncomfortable, they got well; but if, when apparently restored, they were sent back to service, they promptly went sick again. There was nothing to be done with them. And the case is the same with neurotics in civilian life. They complain of their illness, but they make the most of it, and when it comes to taking it away from them they will defend it like a lioness her young; there is no use in reproaching them with their contradiction.

'Then would it not be best not to treat them at all, but leave them to themselves? I cannot see that it is worth while to spend all that time and effort on each individual, which according to you is necessary.'

There I cannot agree. It is certainly better to deal with the complications of life as they are, instead of quarrelling with their existence. Not every neurotic whom we treat may be worth the trouble of analysis, but there are many valuable personalities amongst them. The goal of our achievement must be to secure that so few human beings as possible are left to confront civilised life with such defective psychical equipment; and to that end we must collect much material, and learn to understand much. Every analysis is instructive and can be made to yield fresh elucidation, quite apart from the personal worth of the individual patient.

'But if a determination to retain the illness has been formed in the patient's Ego, it must rest upon some foundations and motives to justify it. I cannot see why a man should want to be ill, or what he gains by it.'

Oh, that is not far to seek. Think of the war-neurotics who escape all service because they are ill. In civilian life illness may be used as a protection—to palliate incapacity at work or among competitors, or in family life as a means to force sacrifices and demonstrations of affection from others, or impose one's will upon them. All this is comparatively on the surface, and we put it all together under the heading 'advantage gained by illness'; the only remarkable thing is that the patient—his Ego—knows nothing of the whole connection of such motives with his resulting behaviour. One combats the influence of these impulses by forcing the Ego to accept this knowledge. But there are still other and deeper-lying motives, with which one cannot be done so easily. To understand these, however, we must make a fresh plunge into psychological theory.

'Go on, by all means. A little more theory can hardly daunt me by now.'

When I set out the relationship of Ego and Id I kept back an important part of the theory of the psychical apparatus. It is this: we were forced to assume that in the Ego itself a special agency has become differentiated, which we name the Super-Ego. This Super-Ego holds a special position between the Ego and the Id. It belongs to the Ego, shares its high psychological organisation, but stands in an especially intimate connection with the Id. It is, actually, the precipitate of the Ego's first attachments to objects; the heir of the Œdipus complex, when that has been vacated. This Super-Ego can set itself against the Ego. It can treat it as an object, and often uses it very harshly. It is just as important for the Ego to live in concord with the Super-Ego as with the Id. Discords between Ego and Super-Ego have great significance for psychical life. You will have guessed by now that the Super-Ego is the vehicle for the phenomenon we call 'conscience'. It is very important for mental health that the Super-Ego should develop normally—that is, that it should become sufficiently depersonalised. It is precisely this that does not happen in the case of a neurotic, because his Œdipus complex does not undergo the right transformation. His Super-Ego deals with his Ego like a strict father with a child, and his idea of morality displays itself in primitive ways by making the Ego submit to punishment by the Super-Ego. Illness is employed as a means for this 'self-punishment'. The neurotic has to behave as though he were mastered by guilt, which the illness serves to punish, and so to relieve him.

'That really does sound very mysterious. The most remarkable thing is that even this power of his conscience should not come into the patient's consciousness.'

Yes, we are only now beginning to appreciate the significance of all these important inter-relations. That is what has made my presentation so difficult. I can now continue. We call all the forces which oppose the work of cure the patient's 'resistances'. The gain from the illness is the source of one resistance, and 'unconscious guilt' represents the resistance from the Super-Ego; this is the most powerful factor, and the one we most fear. We meet still other resistances in the course of the treatmnt. If the Ego, in the early period, undertook a repression on account of anxiety, that anxiety still exists, and now expresses itself as a resistance if the Ego approaches what is repressed. Finally, it may well be imagined that difficulties arise when an instinctual process, which has followed a certain path perhaps for decades, is suddenly required to take a new course which has now opened for it. One might call that the resistance of the Id. The fight against all these resistances is the main work in the treatment, and the task of interpretation seems small beside it. But by this battle with resistances, and their defeat, the patient's Ego, too, will become so altered and strengthened that we may rely upon his behaviour after the treatment is over. On the other hand, you will now see why treatments take so long. Length of preceding development and abundance of material are not the decisive factors. It is rather a question of whether the way is clear. To cover a distance which in peacetime takes a few hours in the train, an army may require weeks, if it has to overcome the resistance of an enemy on the ground. Such battles take time, too, in mental life. I am sorry to say that all efforts to accelerate analytical treatment to any substantial extent have so far miscarried. The best way to shorten it seems to be to carry it out correctly.

'If I felt any inclination to dabble in your craft and even undertake to analyse someone else, your disclosures about resistances have cured me of it. But now, what about the especial personal influence which you admitted to exist? Does it not come up against them?'

It is as well that you raise that now. This personal influence is our strongest dynamic weapon, it is the new factor which we bring to the situation, to make it fluid. The intellectual validity of our explanations cannot achieve that, since the patient shares all the prejudices current in our surrounding world, and may as little believe us as do our scientific critics. The neurotic sets himself to the work because he believes in the analyst, and he believes in him because he begins to entertain certain feelings towards him. A child, too, believes only in the people to whom it is attached. I mentioned before how we employ this peculiar and powerful 'suggestive' influence. Not for the suppression of symptoms—that fact distinguishes the psycho-analytic method from others in psychotherapy—but as an instinctual force to induce the patient's Ego to conquer his resistances.

'Yes, and if you succeed? Is it all smooth going after that?'

It should be. But there is an unexpected complication. It was perhaps the biggest surprise for the analyst of all, to find that the emotional attitude towards him which the patient takes up is of a quite peculiar kind. The first physician who tried an analysis—it was not I—encountered this phenomenon, and did not know what to make of it. The attitude is, in fact—to put it bluntly—a kind of falling in love. Remarkable, is it not,—if you bear in mind that the analyst does nothing to provoke it, but on the contrary rather keeps his distance from the patient and maintains a certain reserve in the matter of ordinary personal relationships; and if you consider further that this surprising love disregards all questions of whether conditions are really favourable, and discounts all variations of personal attraction, or age, sex, or position. This love is in fact *compulsive*. Not that this characteristic need be regarded as otherwise foreign to spontaneous love. You know that the contrary is often the case, but this feature always appears in the analytical situation, without any rational explanation. One would suppose that the relationship between patient and analyst would evoke in the former no more than a certain measure of respect, reliance, gratitude and human liking. Instead of these there is this falling in love, which in itself has an appearance of something pathological.

'Now, I should have thought that would forward your analytical ends. If one is in love one is very compliant, and will do anything for the other person's sake.'

Yes, it is a help at the outset, but later on, when the love has deepened, its whole nature becomes clear and there is much in it which is incompatible with the task of analysis. The patient's love is no longer satisfied to obey; it becomes exacting, demands affectionate and sensual gratification, claims exclusive attention, develops jealousy, and shows ever more clearly its obverse side, its readiness to lapse into hostility and revengefulness if it cannot achieve its ends. At the same time, like every love affair, it pushes all other mental activities out of the way; it wipes out interest in the treatment and in improvement, and in short, we can be in no doubt that it has usurped the place of the neurosis, and our work has had the result of replacing one form of illness by another.

'That seems hopeless. What do you do then? You must have to give up the analysis, but then, if as you say every case falls out like this, you might as well never undertake it.'

We will first try to learn from the situation. What we get in that way may help us to master it. Is it not very noteworthy that we have succeeded in changing a neurosis, with any sort of content you please, into a pathological state of being in love?

Our conviction that a part of abnormally directed love-activity lies at the root of neurosis must receive sure support from this experience. With this insight we can stand firm again, and proceed to take this state of being in love itself as an object for analysis. And we make another observation. This analytical falling in love does not find such clear and indeed glaring expression in all cases as I have suggested. But why? We shall soon see. In measure as the positive and hostile sides of his love emerge, the patient's opposition to them is aroused. He battles with them, tries to repress them, under our eyes. And now we come to understand the process. The patient *repeats*, in the form of falling in love with the analyst, psychical experiences which he underwent before; he has *transferred* to the analyst psychical attitudes which lay ready within him, and which were intimately linked with the inception of his neurosis. He repeats, too, his one-time defence-reactions before our eyes, and wants nothing so much as to repeat all the vicissitudes of that forgotten period in his relations with the analyst. So, what he is showing us is the very core of his most private life; *he is palpably reproducing it, as though it were all happening in the present, instead of remembering it.* With this, the riddle of transference-love is solved, and with the very help of the new situation, which seemed so threatening, the analysis can make progress.

'That is all very subtle. And does the patient find it easy to believe you, when you tell him he is not really in love with you, but merely feels compelled to act something over again?'

Everything depends on that, and the greatest adroitness in handling the 'transference' is required to achieve it. You will see that this point represents the culminating demands upon analytical technique. It is here that one may make the gravest mistakes or achieve the greatest success. It would be senseless to attempt to evade difficulties by suppressing or ignoring the transference; whatever else may have been done up to this point could not deservedly be called an analysis. To send the patient away, so soon as the awkwardnesses of his transference-neurosis came into play, would be absurd, and cowardly as well; it would be as though one were to summon up spirits, and then run away when they appeared. Sometimes, indeed, there is nothing else to be done; there are cases in which the transference, once unleashed, cannot be mastered, and the analysis must then be broken off. But at least one should first do one's utmost in contending with the evil spirits. To yield to the demands arising from the transference, and to satisfy the patient's affectionate or sensual wishes, is out of the question, not only on very proper moral grounds, but because that course would be wholly inappropriate as a technical means to achieve the purpose of the analysis. A neurotic cannot be cured by merely being allowed to re-enact an uncorrected version of what is already unconsciously stereotyped within him. If one compromises, and offers the patient partial satisfaction in exchange for his further collaboration in the work of the analysis, one must take care not to fall into the position of the priest who meant to convert the insurance agent. The agent remained unconverted, but the priest became insured. The only possible way out from the transference-situation is to take it back to the patient's past as he experienced it in reality, or as his wishful phantasy has constructed it. And this requires from the analyst much dexterity, patience, calmness and self-abnegation.

'And where do you make out that a neurotic experienced the prototype of the love he develops in the transference?'

In his childhood, and usually in connection with one of his parents. You remember the importance we had to ascribe to these first emotional relationships. We have now come full circle.

'Have you really finished? My mind is in something of a whirl with all you have told me. But tell me just one thing more. How and where do people learn what is required for the practice of analysis?'

There are at present two Institutes where training in psycho-analysis is given. The first in Berlin, organised and financed by Dr. Max Eitingon for the Berlin Psychoanalytical Society. The second is maintained by the Vienna Society at its own expense, and at considerable sacrifice. So far, the authorities' part in the matter has been confined to putting a variety of difficulties in the way of the young institutions. A third Institute will shortly be opened by the London Society, under the direction of Dr. Ernest Jones. In these Institutes the candidates are themselves analysed, attend lectures on all the theoretical subjects concerned, and have the advantage of supervision by older and more experienced analysts when they undertake their first attempts at analysing comparatively easy cases. It takes about two years to train an analyst. Naturally even then, he or she is only a beginner, not an expert. Remaining deficiencies can only be filled up by the practice of analysis, or by exchange of views in the psycho-analytical societies where the young members can meet older practitioners. The preparation for analytical practice is no simple and easy matter; the work is hard and the responsibility heavy. But, anyone who has undergone such a discipline; has been analysed; has grasped the psychology of the unconscious as it is known to-day; has become versed in the scientific aspects of sexuality; and has learnt the delicate technique of psycho-analysis, the art of interpretation, the way to combat resistances, and to manage the transference—*that person is no longer a layman in the field of psycho-analysis.* He has acquired the ability to undertake the treatment of neurotic disorders, and will be able, in time, to achieve everything which can be hoped for from this form of therapy.

VI

'You have gone to great trouble to explain to me what psycho-analysis is, and what knowledge is required to practise it with any prospect of success. It has certainly done me no harm to listen to you. But I do not see what influence you expect all this to have on my opinion. I regard the case as nothing out of the way. Neuroses are a particular kind of illness, and analysis a particular method of treating them—a medical speciality. It is the practice that a physician who chooses to specialise does not content himself with the qualifications secured with his ordinary medical degree, especially if he wishes to establish himself in a large town—which is the only place to support a specialist. Anyone who wishes to practise as a surgeon tries to spend some years in the surgical department of a hospital, and the same with eye-specialists, ear nose and throat men, and so on; and above all the psychiatrist, who will perhaps spend all his days on the staff of an asylum or private sanatorium. I should expect the same thing for the psycho-analyst too. Anyone who decides for that new medical speciality will at the end of his ordinary studies undertake the two years' course at an Institute which you have mentioned, if indeed it must really take so long. He will then see the advantages of maintaining contact with his colleagues in a psycho-analytical society, and all will go well. I do not see where the question of lay analysis need arise at all.'

The doctor who does what you have promised in his name will always be welcome to us. Four-fifths of those whom I recognise as my pupils are, in fact, qualified physicians. But permit me to explain what the relation-ships of doctors to psycho-analysis have been in practice, and how they are likely to develop. The medical profes-sion has no historical claim to a monopoly in analysis; rather, until recently it has done everything possible to damage it, from shallow sneers to serious calumnies. You may justly say that that belongs to the past and ought not to affect the future. I agree, but I fear that the future will not be as you have predicted it.

Let me use the word 'quack' in its real rather than its legal sense. In the eyes of the law, a quack is one who treats patients without being able to produce a State medical degree. I should prefer another definition: a quack is a person who undertakes a treatment without possessing the knowledge and capacity required for it. On the basis of this definition, I make bold to assert that doctors furnish the largest contingent of quacks in analy-sis—and not only in European countries. They very often use analytical treatment, without having learnt it and without understanding it.

It is vain for you to object that that would be an un-conscionable proceeding of which you would not like to accuse the medical profession. A doctor indeed knows that his medical degree is no letter of marque, and the patient is no outlaw. One should always be able to rely on a doctor's acting in good faith, even if he sometimes makes mistakes.

The facts remain; let us hope that they are open to that explanation. I shall try to set out for you the way in which it becomes possible for a doctor to act in psycho-analytical matters in a way which he would be most careful to avoid in any other field.

In the first place, we must consider the fact that in the medical schools the student's course of instruction is more or less the opposite of what he would need as preparation for psycho-analysis. His attention is directed to objective, verifiable facts of anatomy, physics, and chemistry, and his success in medical practice will depend on his learning them aright and applying them properly. The problem of life is brought into consideration, insofar as it has emerged, up to now, from the play of forces which are demonstrable in inorganic matter also. No interest is evoked in the psychological side of vital phenomena; the study of the higher achievements of the mind is nothing to do with medicine—it comes within the scope of another Faculty. Psychiatry, alone, is concerned with the disturbances of mental functioning; but one knows in what way and with what purposes. Psychiatry looks for the physical causes of mental disorders and treats them like those of any other illness.

It is right that this should be done, and the medical instruction is clearly excellent. If one levels an accusation of one-sidedness, one must submit a reason why this should be a reproach. In itself, every science is one-sided; it must be, because it is confined to certain contents, standpoints, and methods. It would be a piece of absurdity, in which I would wish to have no part, to try to play off one science against another. The value of chemistry is not detracted from by physics; the one cannot replace the other, nor supersede it. Psycho-analysis, indeed, is particularly one-sided, being the science of the unconscious mind. So we need not deny to medicine the right to be one-sided.

But we find the required point of view when we turn from the scientific aspect of medicine to the practical art of healing.. A sick man is a complicated being, and he may serve as a reminder that mental phenomena, difficult to comprehend as they are, cannot be erased from the picture life presents. The neurotic, indeed, is an undesirable complication, an embarrassment to the art of healing not less than to Courts of Justice or the army. Yet he exists, and he is of especially close concern to medicine. But medical training does nothing towards either evaluating his case or treating it—absolutely nothing at all. In view of the intimate connection between what we distinguish as physical and mental we may foresee the day when a path of knowledge, and we may hope influence, may be opened from the biology of organs, and from chemistry, to the phenomenological field of the neuroses. But this day still seems distant, and at present these neurotic conditions are inaccessible from the medical side.

The situation would not be intolerable if medical training simply denied to doctors any approach to the field of neurosis. But it does more; it gives them a false and positively harmful attitude towards it. Doctors, having had no interest aroused in the psychical factors in life, are all too ready to disparage them, and even to treat them as matters for scientific ridicule. For this reason they cannot take the subject seriously, and are insensible to the obligations which flow from it. Thus they fall into a truly lay attitude of disrespect for psychological research, and make their task easy for themselves. Neurotics, indeed, have to be treated, since they are ill and come to the doctor; and one must keep trying something fresh. But why go to the pains of a wearisome training? One can get along; who knows whether what is taught in the psycho-analytical Institutes is any good? The less these doctors understand

of the subject, the more they are ready to do.   Only the
really knowledgeable man is diffident, because he knows
how insufficient his knowledge is.

The comparison of the analytical speciality with other
branches of medicine, which you adduced as a silencer, is
thus not applicable.   In the case of surgery, ophthalm-
ology, etc., the medical school itself affords opportunity
for further training.   The analytical training-institutes
are few in number, young in years, and unauthoritative.
The medical schools have not recognised them, and pay
them no attention. The young doctor, who has had to take
so much on trust from his teachers that he has had little
chance to educate his own judgment, seizes the opportunity at last afforded him to play the critic in a field where
as yet no recognised authority prevails.

Still other circumstances favour his emergence as an
analytical quack.   If he undertook eye operations without
adequate training, the failure of his extractions of cataract
or iridectomies, and the absence of patients, would soon
put an end to his adventure.   But the practice of analysis
is comparatively free from hazard.   The public is accus-
tomed to a usually successful outcome of operations on the
eye, and expects the surgeon to cure them.   But if a
'nerve-specialist' does not cure his patient, nobody won-
ders at it.   One is not used to successful therapy of neurotics, and the nerve-specialist has at least 'taken a lot of
trouble with him'.   There is evidently nothing much to be
done, it will have to be left to nature, or to time.   In the
case of a woman, perhaps menstruation will do it, then
marriage, later the menopause.   In the end, death brings
the real remedy.   And besides, what the medical analyst
has done with his patient is so little striking as to give no
handle for reproach.   He used no instruments and gave no
medicines; he only talked, and tried persuasion or dis-

suasion. That could surely do no harm, especially if he was careful to avoid touching on anything painful or upsetting. The medical analyst who is emancipated from the constraints of strict instruction will certainly not fail to try to improve upon analysis, to draw its fangs and make it acceptable to his patients. And well for him if he stops here, for if he were really to venture to evoke resistances, and then did not know how to deal with them, he might find himself unpopular in earnest.

It must in justice be admitted that an irresponsible analyst does less harm to a patient than an incompetent surgeon. The possible harm is restricted to useless trouble and expense for the patient, and a loss or diminishment of his chances of cure. Further, the reputation of analytical therapy is lowered. All this is certainly very undesirable, but there is no comparison with the dangers incurred from the knife of a surgical quack. In my opinion serious and lasting aggravation of a neurotic illness is not to be feared from incompetent employment of analysis. The disagreeable reactions soon die down. In comparison with the traumas of life which have evoked the illness, the small matter of maltreatment by the doctor hardly counts. All that has happened is that the unapt attempt at therapy has done no good to the patient.

'I have listened to your description of the medical quacks in analysis without interrupting, but not without forming the impression that you are swayed by some hostility towards the medical profession—you have indeed indicated that there is a historical explanation for that. But I will concede you one thing: if analyses are to be undertaken, it must be by people thoroughly trained to do so. And you do not think that physicians who take up analysis will in time come to do what is necessary to possess themselves of the qualifications?'

I fear not. So long as the relations between the medical schools and the analytical institutes remain as they are, doctors will find the temptation to make things easy for themselves too great to resist.

'But you always seem to avoid giving any express opinion on the question of lay analysis. I suspect that your real position is, that because the doctors who want to practise analysis cannot be brought under control, the monopoly of analysis ought to be taken from them to punish them, as a sort of revenge—and this form of medical practice be opened to laymen as well.'

I do not know whether you have correctly divined my motives. Perhaps I may later be able to give you evidence that my point of view is not so partial as you suggest. But I want to lay all my emphasis on this claim : *that no one should practise analysis who has not qualified himself by a proper training*. Whether the person is a doctor or not seems to me of altogether minor importance.

'Then what proposals would you make on that?'

I have not yet come to it, and begin to wonder whether I ever shall do so. I should like to discuss another question here, and by way of introduction touch on a particular matter. It is rumoured that the authorities, on the instigation of the medical profession, mean to prohibit altogether the practice of analysis by laymen. That prohibition would naturally apply also to the non-medical members of the Psycho-analytical Society, who have had an excellent training and have brought themselves through practice to a high level of skill. If the proposal were put into effect, the position would be that persons were prevented from practising who are demonstrably extremely able in it, while it is thrown open to others for whom no such guarantee can be given. That result is not precisely what the legislation might be intended to secure.

This particular problem, however, is neither very important nor very difficult to solve. It only concerns a handful of people who would not suffer much hardship. They would probably go to Germany, where there is no law against them, and their skill would soon find recognition. If it were desired to mitigate the law in their favour, there are precedents for a saver to be inserted. In monarchical Austria, it happened more than once that notorious 'quacks' were authorised *ad personam* to practice medicine in certain spheres, because of their proved ability to do so. These were mostly rustic healers, vouched for by one of the then numerous Archduchesses, but the same must be held permissible for cities and on other, and purely technical guarantees. More important would be the effect on the Vienna Analytical Institute, which from then on could accept no candidate for training from non-medical circles. Thus, yet once more, our country would see the suppression of an intellectual activity which might otherwise grow and spread. I would be the last to pretend to expert knowledge in matters of legislation. But I know enough to see that a tightening-up of our law as to charlatanism would be out of tune with the present tendency to assimilation with German practice, and that to apply this law to psycho-analysis would be something of an anachronism, since when it was enacted analysis had not yet been invented and the especial nature of neurotic disorders was unknown.

I come to the question which seems to me more important to discuss. Is the practice of psycho-analysis a matter in which the authorities ought to intervene, or is it better left to its natural development? I shall not attempt to decide it now, but I take the liberty of propounding it for your consideration. From olden times there has reigned in our country a veritable *furor prohibendi,* a fondness for

tutelage, interference and prohibition which, as we all
know, has not always borne good fruit. It seems as
though in the new, Republican, Austria, this is as yet little
different. We are supposing that you are in a position to
put in a word of weight on the case of psycho-analysis; I
do not know that you would have either the inclination or
the power to withstand the bureaucratic tendencies. I
shall give you my own opinion on the point, for what it is
worth. I think that a mass of regulations and prohibitions
defeats the law. One has only to look around one to see
that where there are only a few prohibitions, they are
observed; but if they are encountered at every turn, people
soon feel they must try to get round them. Further, one
need not be an anarchist to see that laws and ordinances
have no sacred and unimpugnable origin; they are often
inherently inadequate, and seem, or come to seem after a
time, repellent to our sense of justice. Then, in view of
the apathy of those in charge of affairs, there is often no
other way to correct the position created by bad or mis-
directed laws than to break them. Again, it is wise, if one
wishes to retain respect for laws, to refrain from enact-
ments which are difficult to enforce. Several points which
we have mentioned in regard to the practice of analysis
by doctors can be adduced here in respect of lay analysis,
which the law would prohibit. The process of analysis is
very unostentatious; no medicines or instruments are used,
and it consists merely of talking and exchanging information. It would not be easy to convict a lay person of
practising analysis, if he maintained that he only gave
encouragement and good advice, and tried to bring a con-
soling and humane influence to bear in cases where people
seemed to be mentally in need of such help. One could
hardly forbid him that on the mere ground that doctors
sometimes have to do the same.

In English-speaking countries the practices of Christian Science have become very widespread; a kind of dialectical denials of the ills and evil in life by reliance on the teachings of the Christian religion. I will not conceal my opinion that this procedure constitutes a regrettable aberration of the human mind, but who in either America or England would think of prohibiting or penalising it? Do our authorities feel so certain of the right path that they will venture to hinder anyone from 'seeking felicity after his own fashion'? And admitting that many, left to themselves, run into danger and come to harm, would it not be better for Authority to define carefully the fields which ought to be closed, and for the rest so far as possible leave men to learn from their own experience and from each other? Psycho-analysis has come so lately into the world, the mass of mankind are so little familiar with it, the attitude of official science towards it is still so vacillating, that it seems to me premature to interfere with its development by legal regulation. Let us leave the patients themselves to discover that it harms them to seek help in mental matters from those who have not learnt how to give it. Let us inform them and warn them, and we shall have saved ourselves from having to prohibit. On Italian highways the high-tension electricity standards bear the brief and striking notice, *'Chi tocca, muore'*—'who touches, will die'. This is quite enough to govern the behaviour of passers-by in respect of lines hanging slack. The corresponding German warnings are needlessly and almost insultingly verbose: *'Das Berühren der Leitungsdrähte ist, weil lebensgefährlich, strengstens verboten'*— 'To touch the wires is most strictly forbidden, because of danger to life'. Why the prohibition? Anyone who values his life will refrain of his own accord, and anyone

who wants to end it in this way will not ask whether it is
allowed.

'But there are cases which may be appealed to in this
question of lay analysis. I am thinking of the prohibition
on hypnosis by laymen, and the recent prohibiton of
séances and the foundation of spiritualist societies.'

I cannot say that I am an admirer of these measures.
The last one is an undoubted encroachment on intellectual freedom by police interference. I may be acquitted
of any suspicion of entertaining much belief in so-called
occult phenomena, or yearning much for their recognition; but prohibitions will not stifle men's interest in an
alleged mysterious world. On the contrary, great harm
may have been done by closing for impartial investigators
the path to a judgment which might liberate mankind
from the weight of these oppressive possibilities. But
this, too, only applies in Austria. In other countries
' parapsychic' investigation encounters no legal hindrances. Hypnosis is a case rather different from that
of analysis. It is the inducement of an abnormal mental
state, and at the present day is only employed, by laymen,
for purposes of entertainment. Had it fulfilled the first
bright hopes for hypnotic therapy, similar considerations
would have arisen as in the question of analysis. At all
events, the history of hypnosis furnishes a precedent in
another direction for the fate of analysis. When I was a
young demonstrator in neuropathology, physicians in-
veighed violently against hypnosis, calling it a swindle, an
invention of the devil, and a most dangerous procedure.
To-day they have monopolised this same hypnosis and use
it unabashed as a method of investigation; for some nerve
specialists it is even the main weapon of their therapy.

However, I have already said that I do not wish to
assert propositions which depend on a decision whether

legal regulation or a policy of laissez-faire is the right thing in respect of analysis. I know that this is a question of principle, and those who have to decide it are more likely to be swayed by inclination than by argument. I have already said what seems to me to speak for laissez-faire. But if the decision goes the other way, in favour of active interference, then it would seem to me inadequate merely to enact a lame and one-sided measure forbidding analysis to persons who are not doctors. More would be required—prescription of the conditions under which analysts, whoever they may be, may practise; establishment of some authority to say what analysis is and how one must be trained for it, and indeed to provide the facilities for training. Thus it is a matter of either leaving things alone, or bringing order and precision into them; but not of rushing into a complex situation with an isolated prohibition, derived automatically from legislation which has become inadequate.

VII

'Yes, but the question about doctors! I cannot bring
you to discuss our real subject. You always get away
from me. The point we are supposed to be considering is,
whether one ought to reserve the right to practise analysis exclusively to doctors—subject, for all I care, to their
satisfying certain conditions. The majority of doctors are
certainly not analytical quacks, as you have described
them. You yourself say that by far the greater number of
your pupils and adherents are doctors. I have been told
that they by no means share your opinion on the question
of lay analysis. I may naturally assume that as your
pupils they accept your views as to the necessity of sufficient training and so on, and yet they find it compatible
with this to wish to exclude laymen from analytical practice. Is this so, and if so how do you account for it?'

I see that you are well-informed. It is so. Not all, certainly, but a good number of my medical collaborators do
not follow me in this point, and think that analytical treatment of neurotics should be reserved to medical practitioners. You will observe from this that there can be
differences of opinion in our camp, too. It is known which
side I am on, and the difference over lay analysis means
no breach in our general harmony. You ask me to explain their attitude? I am by no means certain, but I

think it is something to do with professional feeling. They have followed a different line of development from mine; they still feel discomfort in isolation from their colleagues, they would greatly like to be ackonwedged by the profession, and are prepared in exchange for this to offer a sacrifice which to them does not seem vital. This may not be so. To ascribe to them motives connected with competition would be to impute not only base motives but a remarkable shortsightedness. They are indeed always ready to train other doctors in analysis, and for their material interests it cannot matter whether the available patients are shared with medical colleagues or lay practitioners. But probably something else still is involved. These pupils of mine may be influenced by certain factors which assure to a doctor an undoubted advantage over a layman, in analytical practice.

'An advantage! Now we have it. So you do admit an advantage? That should settle the question at last.'

I do not feel difficulty in admitting it. It may show you that I am not so painfully blind as you seem to assume. I have postponed mentioning this circumstance because its discussion requires yet another excursion into theory.

'What now?'

First, there is the question of diagnosis. If one is to take a patient for analytical treatment, who suffers from so-called nervous disorders, one wants first to be certain—so far as certainty is possible—that he is a suitable case for such treatment, and that therefore one can help him by using it. But that is only the case, if he really has a neurosis.

'I should have thought one would know that from appearances—from the symptoms he complains of.'

There is a fresh complication at this point. One can never know for certain. The patient may exhibit the outward picture of a neurosis, and yet it may be something else—the beginning of an incurable mental disease, or of a destructive process in the brain. Distinguishing—differential diagnosis—is not always easy, nor immediately possible at every phase. Responsibility for this must of course rest entirely in medical hands. The physician's task as I say is not always easy. Mental disease may present a harmless appearance for a long time, until suddenly its serious nature becomes apparent. It is indeed a common fear among neurotics—that they may become insane. If a doctor fails to recognise a case of incipient disease for a time, or remains in doubt over it, it does not much matter; no harm and nothing superfluous has been done. Analytical treatment would certainly have done the patient no harm either, but would have been exposed as unnecessary expenditure of money and time. Besides, plenty of people would be found to lay the eventual bad outcome to the charge of the analysis. Unjustly so, certainly, but such occasions are best avoided.

'But this seems hopeless. It destroys by the roots everything that you have told me about the nature and rise of a neurosis.'

Not at all. It merely reinforces the fact that neurotics are a nuisance and a difficulty to all parties, including the analyst. Perhaps I shall set your worries at rest again if I express myself more correctly. It is probably more correct to say, as regards the cases we have just been considering, that they have actually developed a neurosis, but it is not psychogenic but somatogenic—its causes are not mental but physical. Can you understand me?

'Understand, yes; but I cannot reconcile this with the other—the psychological side.'

That can be done, if only we will take into account the complexity of living substance. What did we regard as the essence of a neurosis? The fact that the Ego, the more highly organised part of the mental apparatus bred up under the influence of the outer world, is not in a position to fulfil its function of mediation between Id and reality; that in its weakness it retreats from some part of the instinctual activity of the Id; and suffers the consequences of this renunciation in the form of contractions of its influence, symptoms, and unsuccessful reaction-formations.

In all of us, the Ego was weak in this way during childhood; that is why the events of our earliest years have such significance for later life. An extraordinary burden is laid on childhood. In a very few years we have to traverse the immense evolutionary distance from the Stone Age to participation in modern civilisation, and therewith in particular to parry the instinctual impulses of the early sexual period. Under this burden our Ego takes refuge in repressions, and exposes itself to a childhood neurosis, the precipitate of which it carries forward as a predisposition to later neurotic disturbance in maturity. Then all depends on how fate treats the individual as he grows older. If life is too harsh, the difference between the demands of instinct and the exactions of the outside world too great, the Ego may come to grief in its efforts to reconcile the two; the more so, the more it is inhibited by the disposition brought from childhood. It then repeats the process of repression, the instincts tear themselves free from its mastery and create their substitute-satisfactions along the path of regression; the poor Ego has become helplessly neurotic.

Let us stick to this—that the pivotal point in the whole situation is the relative strength of the organisation of the Ego. We can then easily complete our aetiological picture. We already know the, so to speak, normal causes of

F

neuroticism: the task of mastering the early impulses of sexuality, and the effects of childhood experiences which òccur in a more chance way. But is it not possible, too, that other factors, originating before childhood, play a part? For example, an inborn strength and indomitability of the unconscious instinctual life of the Id, which sets too great a task for the Ego from the very outset? Or an especial weakness in the Ego's capacity to develop, for reasons unknown? Obviously such factors must have some aetiological significance, in some cases a decisive one. We must always take account of the strength of the instincts in the Id. Where this has grown to be excessive, the prognosis for our therapy is bad. As to the cause of inhibition of development of the Ego, we know too little as yet. All these, then, would be cases of neurosis based essentially on constitutional factors. Probably, indeed, no neurosis occurs without some such constitutional, congenital predisposition.

If however, the relative weakness of the Ego is the determining factor for the occurrence of neurosis, it must also be possible that a later physical illness may produce a neurosis, if it in fact brings about a weakening of the Ego. And this is very often the case. A somatic disturbance may affect the instinctual activity in the Id, and increase the strength of the instincts beyond the limits to which the Ego is matched. One might take as a normal pattern of such processes the modification which takes place in women during the disturbances of menstruation and the menopause. Or a general disease of the body, let alone an organic disease of the central nervous system, may attack the sources of nutrition of the psychical apparatus, forcing it to function on a lower plane and suspend its more refined activities, among them the maintenance of the Ego-organisation. All these cases present more or less the same picture, of neurosis; neurosis has always the same psychological mechanism, but, as we have seen, the aetiology is highly varied and often most complex.

'Now I am better pleased with you. You have spoken at last like a physician. And I anticipate that you will admit, now, that a thing so medically complicated as a neurosis can only be handled by a physician.'

I am afraid you have overshot the mark. What we have just discussed is a piece of pathology; analysis is a therapeutic procedure. I allow—no, I insist, that every case where an analysis may be required shall first be diagnosed by a physician. The neuroses of the majority of those who come to us are fortunately psychogenic, and there is no question of pathological elements. Once this has been established by the physician, we may safely leave the analytical treatment to the lay analyst. This has always been the procedure in our psycho-analytical societies. Thanks to the intimate contact between medical and non-medical members the mistakes which might have been feared have been to all intents and purposes ruled out. There may be a second stage at which the analyst must seek the help of a physician. In the course of the treatment symptoms—usually physical symptoms—may appear, which the analyst may be doubtful whether to regard as originating entirely from the neurosis, or caused by an organic disturbance arising independently of it. This, too, must be decided by the physician.

'Then the lay analyst cannot dispense with the physician even during the analysis. Another argument against him.'

No, this eventuality provides no argument against the lay analyst, for if it arose for a medical analyst he would have to act in the same way.

F *

'I do not follow that.'

It is a rule of technique that if such doubtful symptoms appear during an analysis, the analyst must not rely on his own judgment, but must refer the case to a physician having nothing to do with the analysis—even when he himself is a physician and has retained confidence in his medical opinion.

'And why is this laid down? It seems to me unnecessary.'

It is not unnecessary; there are several reasons for it. Firstly, organic and psychical treatments do not go well together in the same hands; secondly, while the transference prevails it may make it inadvisable for the analyst to examine the patient physically; and thirdly, the analyst has every ground to mistrust his own objectivity, since his interest is so closely enlisted in the psychical factors.

'Your position on lay analysis is now clear to me. You are determined that at all costs there must be lay analysts. And since you cannot contest their inadequacy for their task, you bring in everything which may serve as an excuse for them, and make things easier for them. But I myself cannot see why lay analysts are wanted; at best they can only be therapeutists of the second class. I am willing to except the few lay people who have already trained as analysts, but I do not think any new ones should be made, and the Institutes ought to undertake that they will accept no more for training.'

I will agree with you, if you can show that such a restriction will serve the interests of all concerned. You will concede that these are of three kinds—those of the patients, of the doctors, and, last but not least, of scientific knowledge, which includes the interest of all future patients. May we consider these in turn?

So far as the patient is concerned, it does not matter whether the analyst is a doctor or not, so long as the danger of a mistake as to his case is secured against by the prescribed medical opinion before the analysis begins, and, if required, during its course. For him, it is incomparably more important that the analyst should possess such personal qualities as will command his confidence, and that he should have acquired the knowledge and insight, and the experience, which alone can fit him for his task. One might imagine that the analyst's prestige would be lowered in the patient's eyes by the knowledge that he is not a doctor and in some situations must have recourse to a doctor. Naturally, we have never neglected to inform patients as to the analyst's qualifications, and we have become convinced that professional prejudice finds no echo in them—they are ready to accept a cure from wherever it is offered, as, incidentally, the medical profession has long been acutely and resentfully aware. Lay analysts, as they are found practising to-day, are not chance-comers, recruited and trained without discrimination, but persons of academic standing, Doctors of Philosophy, teachers and a number of women of wide experience and exceptional personality. The analysis which all candidates at a psycho-analytical institute are required to undergo is, at the same time, the best way to form conclusions as to their personal aptitude for the exacting profession they have chosen.

Next, as to the interest of physicians. I cannot believe that medicine stands to gain from the incorporation of psycho-analysis. The medical course now takes five years, with the final examinations taking up much of the sixth. Every few years new requirements appear for the student and if he does not fulfil them he will face the future inadequately equipped. Entry to the medical profession is a very difficult matter, and its practice brings neither great satisfaction nor great material reward. If one were to insist on the very tenable point of view that a doctor ought to be relied on to deal, too, with the mental side of illness, and so stretched the medical education to include partial training for analysis, it would mean a substantial increase in what has to be learnt and a corresponding extension of the student years. I do not know that doctors would be pleased at such a consequence of their claim to monopolise psycho-analysis. But it is scarcely to be avoided. And this, at a time when material conditions have worsened so much for the class from which doctors are recruited, that the younger generation is compelled to become self-supporting so soon as possible.

Perhaps, however, you would wish not to burden the medical curriculum with preparation for analytical practice, but think it more appropriate that future analysts should not trouble themselves with the required training until they have completed their medical studies. You may say that the time so lost hardly matters, because a young man of under thirty cannot enjoy that confidence from patients which is required if a mental cure is to be effected. To that it might be answered that the newly-qualified doctor for bodily ailments cannot count, either, upon great respect from patients; and that the young analyst could very well fill in his time by working in a psycho-analytical clinic under the supervision of experienced practitioners.

What seems more important to me is the fact that by such a prescription you are imposing a squandering of effort which in these difficult times cannot in fact be justified on economic grounds. Analytical training certainly intersects the circle of medical training, but it does not comprise it nor is it comprised within it. If a psycho-

analytical faculty were to be set up—a notion which may
to-day seem a phantasy—much would have to be taught
in it which is also taught in a medical faculty. Besides
depth-psychology, i.e. the psychology of the unconscious,
which will always be the main subject, some biology
would be required, the science of sex in its widest sense,
and some knowledge of the clinical pictures dealt with in
psychiatry. On the other hand, the analytical curriculum
would include subjects which are far removed from medicine and which a doctor would never require in his practice: the history of civilisation, mythology, the psychology
of religion, and literature. Unless he is well oriented in
these fields the analyst will be unable to bring understanding to bear upon much of his material. And, vice versa,
he can find no use for the greater part of what is taught
in medical schools. A knowledge of the anatomy of the
metatarsal bones, of the properties of carbo-hydrates, of
the courses of the cranial nerves, of all that medicine has
discovered as to bacillary infection and means to prevent
it, or of serum reactions, or neoplasms—all this is of the
greatest value in itself, but will take him nowhere. It will
not directly help him to understand and cure a neurosis,
nor does this sort of knowledge sharpen the intellectual
faculties on which his professional activity will make such
demands. The analyst's experience lies in another world
from that of pathology, with other phenomena and other
laws. However philosophy may bridge the gap between
physical and mental, it still exists for practical purposes,
and our practice on each side of it must differ accordingly.

It would be unjust and inappropriate to force a man,
bent upon liberating another from the suffering caused by
a phobia or obsession, to take the long way round of
medical qualification. And it would be of no effect, unless
to suppress analysis altogether. Imagine two paths to

some vantage-point with a beautiful view—one short and
direct, the other long and devious. You wish to close the
short one by a notice—perhaps because it leads through
flowers which you wish to preserve. Your prohibition will
only be effective if the short way is steep and difficult, and
the long one easy and agreeable. If it is the other way
about, we can foresee the effectiveness of your notice, and
the fate of your flowers. I fear that you can as little force
laymen to study medicine as I could persuade doctors to
learn analysis. You know what human nature is.

'If you are right in all this; if analytical practice requires special training, which it is too much to add to the
medical curriculum, and if in any event the medical course
is largely superfluous for an analyst,—what becomes of
the notion of the ideal physician, equal to all the demands
of his calling.'

I cannot foresee the way out of those difficulties, and
I am not the person to find one. I see just two things—
first, that you regard analysis as an embarrassment, and
would prefer that it did not exist. The neurotic, of
course, is an embarrassment too. Second, that for the
present all interests would be served if the medical profession would decide to tolerate a class of therapeutists
who relieve them of the burdensome treatment of the
enormous number of psychogenic neuroses, and who
remain constantly in touch with them, to the great advantage of the patients.

'Is that your last word, or have you something more to
say?'

I wanted to deal with the third interest involved, that
of scientific knowledge. What I have to say on that may
not concern you greatly, but it means much to me.

We do not want to see psycho-analysis swallowed up by
medicine, and then to find its last resting-place in text-

books on psychiatry—in the chapter headed 'Therapy', next to procedures such as hypnotic suggestion, auto-suggestion, and persuasion, which were created out of our ignorance, and owe their short-lived effectiveness to the laziness and cowardice of the mass of mankind. Psycho-analysis deserves a better fate, and it is to be hoped it will have one. As 'psychology of the depths', the theory of the unconscious mind, it may become indispensable to all the branches of knowledge having to do with the origins and history of human culture and its great institutions; such as art, religion, and the social order. It has already con-tributed to the solution of problems in these fields, but the contribution made is small in comparison with what it will be when historians of civilisation, psychologists of religion, etymologists, etc., become willing to use the new weapon for research themselves. Therapy of neuroses is only one of the uses of analysis; perhaps the future will show that it is not the most important. At all events, it would be unreasonable to sacrifice all other uses to this one, merely because it touches the field of professional medicine.

For, at this point, a chain of connection is unrolled which any interference must damage. If the exponents of the various branches of mental science wish to learn psycho-analysis, so as to apply its methods and points of view to their material, it is not enough for them merely to read what is recorded in analytical literature. They must come to understand analysis by the only possible way, that is, by undergoing an analysis themselves. Thus there is to be added, to the neurotics who need analysis, a second class of persons who undergo it from intellectual motives, but who will certainly also derive a welcome advantage from the increased ability which analysis will procure to them incidentally. For these analyses a number of analysts will be needed for whom knowledge of medicine would have especially small significance. But these—teaching-analysts as we might call them—must undergo an especially careful training. If their scope is not to be too restricted, they must be given the opportunity to gain experience from instructive and convincing cases, and since healthy people not in search of special knowledge do not seek analysis, it can once again only be neurotics on whom the teacher-analyst (under most careful supervision) may learn what he needs for the non-medical work he will later do. All this requires freedom and flexibility, with no petty interferences.

Possibly you may think little of these purely theoretical considerations, or you may not think they should influence the practical question of lay analysis. In that case, let me mention yet another field of application for psychoanalysis, quite outside the scope of the law as to 'quackery', and where medical claims can hardly arise. I am referring to education. If a child shows signs of undesirable development, if it becomes moody, stubborn, and inattentive, the doctor can do nothing for it—and this, even if it produces clearly neurotic symptoms, such as anxiety, anorexia, vomiting, and insomnia. A treatment combining analytical influence with educational measures, undertaken by persons who are not above occupying themselves with a child's world and who understand how to get at its mind, will effect two things; it will eliminate the nervous symptoms and undo the malformation of character which has begun. In view of what we know as to the significance of childhood neuroses, often unobtrusive at the time, in predisposing to serious illness in later life, we must regard analysis of children as an excellent method of prophylaxis. Analysis undoubtedly has its enemies: I do not know what means they could adopt to stop the activity of such pedagogic analysts or analyst-pedagogues, and I do not think it would be easy to do so. But, indeed, one should never feel too confident on such a matter.

For the rest, to return to our question of the analytical treatment of adults, we are still not at the end of the considerations involved. Our civilisation puts an almost intolerable pressure on us, and some alleviating correction is wanted. Is it only a phantasy to hope that analysis, in spite of all its difficulties, might be called in to prepare mankind to find and apply such a corrective? Perhaps one day it will occur to some American millionaire to apply part of his fortune to provide analytical schooling for the social workers of his country, and so mobilise a corps to give battle to the neuroses springing from our civilisation.

'Aha, a new sort of Salvation Army!'

Why not? Our phantasy always works on existing patterns. The stream of workers eager for knowledge, which would then flow to Europe, would have to pass Vienna by, since analytical development here may have died as a consequence of early traumatic intervention. You smile? I do not say it to influence your judgment—far from it. I know that you do not believe me, and I cannot tell for certain how things will turn out. But this I do know: it is not so vastly important what decision you may come to on the question of lay analysis. That may have a local effect. But the matter from which the question arises, the possibilities of development inherent in psycho-analysis,—no ordinances and prohibitions will succeed against these.